LONDON'S
FIRE
STATIONS

LONDON'S FIRE STATIONS

John B. Nadal

JM

JEREMY MILLS
PUBLISHING LIMITED

Published by Jeremy Mills Publishing Limited

The Red House, 22 Occupation Road, Lindley,
Huddersfield, UK, HD3 3BD

www.jeremymillspublishing.co.uk

First published 2006

ISBN 0-9546484-7-1

Book design and typesetting by Paul Buckley

Printed by Replika Press Pt Ltd

Westminster fire station c1906. The appliances shown are typical of the time, a horse drawn steamer with coachmen and crew, a horse drawn wheeled escape with coachman and crew and two firemen with a hose cart. These are listed alongside the photos within the book and will be able to give you a mental picture of them when viewing the photos.

Contents

Acton… Gunnersbury Lane W3	Page 189
Addington… Lodge Lane Croydon	Page 198
Barbican… Moore Lane City of London	Page 168
Barking… Alfred's Way	Page 185
Barnet /1… Leicester Road	Page 176
Barnet /2… Station Road	Page 224
Battersea /1… Simpson Street SW11	Page 83
Battersea/2… Este Road SW11	Page 166
Battersea Sub Stn… Battersea Park Road SW11	Page 121
Battersea River… Battersea Bridge Road SW11	Page 130
Bayswater… Pickering Place Westminster	Page 141
Beckenham /1… Bromley Road	Page 175
Beckenham /2… Beckenham Road	Page 217
Belsize… Lancaster Grove NW3	Page 160
Bethnal Green /1… 51 Green Street E2	Page 117
Bethnal Green /2… Roman Road E2	Page 209
Bexley /1… Brampton Road Bexleyheath	Page 182
Bexley /2… Erith Eoad Bexleyheath	Page 210
Biggin Hill… Kingsmead	Page 192
Bishopsgate… Bishopsgate EC3	Page 94
Blackheath… Tranquil Vale Brigade Street SE3	Page 81
Bow / 1… Glebe Road Poplar	Page 72
Bow /2… Parnell Road E3	Page 158
Bow / 3… Parnell Road E3	Page 214
Brixton /1… Shepherds Lane SW9	Page 72
Brixton /2… Gresham Road SW9	Page 149
Bromley… South Street	Page 177
Brompton… South Parade SW3	Page 118
Brunswick Road… Brunswick Road E14	Page 155
Burdett Road… Burdett Road E3	Page 142
Caledonian Road… Copenhagen Street N1	Page 155
Camberwell… Peckham Road SE5	Page 71
Camden Town… St Pancras Way NW1	Page 95
Cannon Street… Cannon Street EC4	Page 150
Chandos Street… Chandos Street WC2	Page 59
Charlton… Charlton Road SR7	Page 153
Chelsea /1… Pavilion Road SW1	Page 90
Chelsea /2… King's Road SW3	Page 206
Cherry Garden River… Cherry Gardens SE16… see Rotherhithe	Page 120
Chingford… The Ridgeway	Page 193
Chiswick… Sutton Lane W4	Page 204
Clapham /1… Old Town SW4	Page 75
Clapham /2… Old Town SW4	Page 136
Clapham /3… Old Town SW4	Page 167
Clerkenwell… Rosebery Avenue EC1	Page126/127
Croydon… Old Town Croydon	Page 198
Dagenham… Rainham Road	Page 189
Deptford /1… Evelyn Street SE8	Page 81
Deptford /2… Evelyn Street SE8	Page 140
Dockhead… Wolseley Street SE1	Page 162
Dowgate… Upper Thames Street EC4	Page 216
Downham /1… Reigate Road Bromley	Page 163
Downham /2… Reigate Road Bromley	Page 226

Dulwich... Lordship Lane SE22   Page 118
Ealing... Uxbridge Road W13   Page 184
East Greenwich /1... Woolwich Road SE7   Page 132
East Greenwich /2... Woolwich Road SE7   Page 218
East Ham... High Street South E6   Page 195
Edgware Road... Edgware Road   Page 130
Edmonton... Church Street N9   Page 192
Eltham... Eltham High Street SE9   Page 143
Enfield... Carterhatch Lane Enfield   Page 207
Erith... Eruth Road Belvedere   Page 199
Euston /1... Euston Road NW1   Page 134
Euston /2... Euston Road NW1   Page 134
Feltham... Faggs Road Feltham   Page 196
Finchley... North Circular Road N3   Page 186
Forest Hill... Stanstead Road SE23   Page 212
Foxley Road... Foxley Road SW9   Page 156
Fulham /1adder & escape shed... North End Road   Page 124
Fulham sub station... North End Road   Page 124
Fulham... Fulham Road SW6   Page 123
Gt.Marlborough Street... Gt Marlborough Street W1   Page 98
Greenwich /1... Lindsell Street SE10   Page 89
Greenwich /2... Blissett Street SE10   Page 167
Hackney /1... Bodney Road E8   Page 73
Hackney /2... Bodney Road E8   Page 159
Hainault... New North Road Hainault   Page 193
Hammersmith /1... Brook Green Lane Hammersmith   Page 85
Hammersmith /2... Shepherds Bush Road W6   Page 159
Hammersmith /3... Shepherds Bush Road W6   Page 229
Hampstead... Heath Street NW3   Page 79
Harrow... Pinner Road Pinner   Page 188
Hayes... Shepiston Lane Harlington   Page 199
Heathrow... Northern Perimeter Road HAL   Page 226
Hendon... The Burroughs NW4   Page 180
Herne Hill... Milkwood Road SE24   Page 147
Heston... London Road Isleworth   Page 187
Highbury... Blackstock Road N5   Page 135
Hillingdon... Uxbridge Road Hillingdon   Page 203
Holborn... Theobolds Road WC1   Page 91
Holloway /1... Mayton Street N7   Page 82
Holloway /2... Hornsey Road N7   Page 154
Holloway /3... Hornsey Road N7   Page 215
Holly Bush Hill (Hampstead)   Page 79
Homerton/1... Homerton High Street E9   Page 133
Homerton/2... Homerton High Street E9   Page 213
Hornchurch... North Street Hornchurch   Page 204
Hornsey... Park Avenue N8   Page 201
Hornsey Rise... Calverly Grove N19   Page 152
Ilford /1... Ley Street Ilford   Page 176
Ilford /2... High Road Ilford   Page 222
Isle of Dogs /1... West Ferry Road E14   Page 88
Isle of Dogs /2... West Ferry Road E14   Page 145
Islington /1... Upper Street N1   Page 131
Islington /2... Upper Street N1   Page 225
Kennington /1... Renfrew Road SE11   Page 75
Kennington /2... Renfrew Road SE11   Page 121
Kensington /1... King Street   Page 80
Kensington /2... Old Court Place W8   Page 144
Kentish Town /1... Fortess Walk NW5   Page 93
Kentish Town /2... Highgate Road NW5   Page 213
Kilburn... Maida Vale NW6   Page 141
Kingsland Road /1... Kingsland Road E8   Page 122
Kingsland Road /1 alt... Kingsland Road E8   Page 122
Kingsland... Kingsland Road E8   Page 215
Kingston... Richmond Road Kingston   Page 194

Knightsbridge /1… Chapel Place SW7	Page 88
Knightsbridge /2… Basil Street SW3	Page 152
Lambeth HQ… Albert Embankment SE1	Page 164
Lambeth River Station/1… Albert Embankment SE1	Page 165
Lambeth River Station/2… Albert Embankment SE1	Page 223
Lee Green /1 Sub Stn… Lee High Road SE12	Page 128
Lee Green /2… Eltham Road SE12	Page 148
Lewisham /1… Lewisham High Street SE13	Page 129
Lewisham /2… Lewisham High Street SE13	Page 208
Leyton /1… Church Road E10	Page 179
Leyton /2… Church Road E10	Page 224
Leytonstone… High Road E11	Page 178
London Salvage Corps… (text reference)	Page 68
Malden… Malden Road	Page 174
Manchester Square… Chiltern Street W1	Page 116
Map LFEE 1833	Page 7
Map LFEE 1865	Page 58
Map MFB	Page 64
Map LCC	Page 115
Map GLC	Page 167
Map LFCDA	Page 220
Map LFEPA	Page 228
Mile End /1… Mile End Road E1	Page 82
Mile End /2… Mile End Road E1	Page 137
Millwall /1… West Ferry Road E14	Page 145
Millwall /2… Bynge Street E14	Page 229
Mill Hill… Hartley Avenue NW7	Page 181
Mitcham… London Road Mitcham	Page 181
New Cross /1… Queen's Road SE14	Page 119
New Cross /1 alt… Queen's Road SE14	Page 120
New Malden… Burlington Road	Page 216
Norbury… London Road	Page 212
North Kensington /1… Faraday Road W10	Page 93
North Kensington /2… Ladbroke Road W10	Page 219
North Woolwich Sub stn… Albert Road E16	Page 129
Northcote Road… Northcote Road SW11	Page 147
Northolt… Petts Hill Northolt	Page 201
Notting Hill… Ladbroke Road W10	Page 76
Old Kent Road /1… Old Kent Road SE1	Page 74
Old Kent Road /2… Old Kent Road SE1	Page 138
Old Kent Road /3… Old Kent Road SE1	Page 210
Orpington… Avalon Road Orpington	Page 194
Paddington /1… Hermitage Street	Page 78
Paddington see –(changed to Edgware Road)	Page 130
Paddington /2… Harrow Road W2	Page 211
Pageant's Wharf… Rotherhithe Street SE16	Page 137
Park Royal… Waxlow Road NW10	Page 196
Peckham /1… Peckham Road SE5	Page 162
Peckham /2… Peckham Road SE5	Page 223
Perry Vale… Perry Vale SE23	Page 133
Plaistow… Prince Regent Lane E13	Page 183
Plumstead… Lakeside Road SE18	Page 151
Poplar /1… West India Dock Road E14	Page 77
Poplar /2… East India Dock Road E14	Page 211
Portland Road… Charlotte Street W1	Page 76
Purley… Brighton Road Purley	Page 182
Redcross Street… Redcross Street EC1	Page 131
Richmond… Lower Richmond Road	Page 203
Romford… Pettits Lane North	Page 197
Rotherhithe… see Cherry Gardens river Stn	Page 120
Rotherhithe… Gomm Road SE16	Page 85
Ruislip… Bury Street Ruislip	Page 200
Rushey Green… Rushey Green SE6	Page 73
St.John's Wood… Adelaide Road Hampstead	Page 80

Sanderstead... Limpsfield Road Sanderstead   Page 188
Scotland Yard... Gt Scotland Yard SW1   Page 92
Shadwell /1... Glamis Road E1   Page 92
Shadwell /2... Cable Street E1   Page 165
Shepherds Bush... Uxbridge Road W12   Page 135
Shooters Hill /1... Shooters Hill SE18   Page 89
Shooters Hill /2... Eaglesfield Road SE18   Page 158
Shoreditch /1... Tabernacle Street EC1   Page 125
Shoreditch /2... Old Street EC1   Page 168
Sidcup... Main Road Sidcup   Page 178
Silvertown /1... North Woolwich Road E16   Page 178
Silvertown /2... North Woolwich Road E16   Page 209
Soho /1... Shaftsbury Avenue W1   Page 161
Soho post war... Shaftsbury Avenue W1   Page 161
Soho /2... Shaftsbury Avenue W1   Page 217
Southall... High Street Southall   Page 206
Southgate... High Street N14   Page 200
Southwark /1... Southwark Bridge Road SE1   Page 86
Southwark /2... Southwark Bridge Road SE1   Page 157
Southwark HQ... Southwark Bridge Road SE1   Page 87
Southwark Street... Southwark SE1   Page 74
Stanmore... Honeypot Lane Stanmore   Page 197
Stoke Newington /1... Leswin Road N16   Page 96
Stoke Newington /2... Stoke Newington Church Street N16   Page 214
Stratford... Romford Road E15   Page 205
Streatham /2... Mitcham Lane SW16   Page 139
Streatham /1 (Sub station)... Mitcham Lane SW16   Page 138
Streatham post war... Mitcham Lane SW16   Page 139
Surbiton... Ewell Road Surbiton   Page 183
Sutton... St Dustan's Hill By Pass Sutton   Page 202
Sydenham... Crystal Palace Parade SE19   Page 77
Thornton Heath... Brigstock Road   Page 179
Tooley Street... Southwark SE1   Page 90
Tooting /1... Balham High Road SW17   Page 78
Tooting /2... Trinity Road SW17   Page 153
Tottenham... St Loy's Road N17   Page 207
Twickenham... South Road   Page 195
Vauxhall... Albert Embankment SW1   Page 136
Wallington... Belmont Road   Page 190
Walthamstow... Forest Road E17   Page 180
Wandsworth /1... West Hill SW18   Page 117
Wandsworth /2... West Hill SW18   Page 166
Wapping... Red Lion Street E1   Page 142
Waterloo /1... Waterloo Road SE1   Page 60
Waterloo /2... Waterloo Road SE1   Page 156
Watling Street HQ... Watling Street EC4   Page 59
Wembley... Harrow Road   Page 191
Wennington... Wennington Road Rainham   Page 202
West Hampstead... West End Lane NW6   Page 132
West Norwood /1... Norwood High Street SE27   Page 91
West Norwood /2... Norwood Road SE27   Page 160
Westminster /1... Francis Street SW1   Page 71
Westminster /2(see frontispiece)... Greycoat Place SW1   Page 146
West Wickham... Glebe Way   Page 190
Whitechapel /1... Commercial Road E1   Page 84
Whitechapel /2... Commercial Road E1   Page 163
Whitefriars... Carmelite Street EC4   Page 128
Willesden... Pound Lane NW10   Page 185
Wimbledon /1... Queen's Road SW19   Page 175
Wimbledon /2... Kingston Road SW19   Page 222
Woodford /1... Snakes Lane   Page 174
Woodford /2... Snakes Lane   Page 225
Woodside... Long Lane Croydon   Page 184
Woolwich... Sunbury Street SE18   Page 97

Foreword

LONDON'S Fire Stations is at once a fascinating historical guide to the London Fire Brigade and a significant commentary on the design and architecture of municipal buildings. The changes in style reflect the political and financial position of the time and it is undoubtedly a wonderful opportunity to ponder the influence that various different authorities brought to bear and their impact not only on the Fire Service, but also the community at large.

John has spent many hours (years!) researching his subject, and I know that his enthusiasm for the project was all-consuming and in many ways infectious to those of us around him. I was privileged to look through the format and content of the book as it went into production and I realised that he had indeed captured the very essence of the service in a quite unique way.

There's nothing quite like a fire station. They come in all shapes and sizes. Some date from a time when firemen and their families lived there too. Some were built to house horse-drawn fire appliances, while others have been designed to meet the changing demands that the 21st century will bring to the fire service.

London's fire stations are much more than a place of work. They are an office, a kitchen, a dining room, a dormitory, a rest area, a gymnasium and a garage rolled into one. Each has its own character, reinforced by the variety of men and women who work, sleep and eat there, 24 hours a day, 365 days a year.

I started London Fire Brigade life as a firefighter at Islington fire station and served in several others during my career. I know, as every firefighter does, that there are places where the bonds formed by the very nature of work that firefighters do are cemented, places where you will find compassion, humour, dignity and above all, a pride in knowing that they are there to serve London and its people and make our capital city a safer place in which to live and work.

Brian Robinson C.B.E. Q.F.S.M.
Chief Officer of the London Fire Brigade 1991-2003

Introduction

DURING my time in the London Fire Brigade as a firefighter I happened across the idea of a book on fire stations and actually started by visiting the Greater London Council (GLC) archives at the old County Hall on the Embankment, where I found boxes of old photos of fire stations. I then contacted the Brigade for permission to use their library but found that at the time it was being relocated and I would be unable to see any photos. This at the time stopped me in my tracks and for some time stopped any further research on London fire stations. Following the demise of the GLC all the records were moved to Clerkenwell to the Greater London Records Office (GLRO) now known as London Metropolitan Archives. It was here that I found the early council records and maps. This rekindled my enthusiasm for a book again. I eventually got to the brigade library and found the photos of the stations and, along with those from other sources, including several of my collection are here in this book. I also visited the Brigade Museum at Winchester House at Southwark where I researched the old books held in their archives, some going as far back as the LFEE (The London Fire Engine Establishment) and some information that would bring it to almost the present time.

In this book you will see the photos of most of the old fire stations past, although many have not survived, some demolished and replaced by a new fire station on the same site. Indeed there are a lot of old stations still about London, some still recognisable, others not so as the appliance doors are often removed and filled in with windows.

The photos are of all of the present fire stations in use by the brigade, pre GLC those of the old MFB the Metropolitan Fire Brigade, LCC London County Council and those absorbed into the brigade during the setting up of the then GLC Greater London Council.

New stations opened during the time of the LFCDA, (The London Fire & Civil Defence Authority), and now of the LFEPA, (London Fire & Emergency Planning Authority) are included.

Maps show locations of stations including those early ones of the LFEE. Although there are no photos to back them up it is surprising where there were fire stations in London all those years ago.

In this book are black and white as well as colour photos, which I hope you will enjoy as much as I have collecting them. The dates shown beside each photo give either the year building completed or when station occupied, other dates show the establishment at the time when published 1892, 1908, 1965 and those of 2005. During the early days of the Fire brigade the firemen lived on station either with his family or in single men's quarters. When the shift system was introduced allowing men to live away from the station the establishment is shown as per watch.

The appliance allocation to stations and the personnel is from information that I have obtained but may possibly in some case now have changed especially during 2005 when many appliance moves occurred. Please except my apologies for any errors.

J.B. Nadal

Chapter 1

London Fire Engine Establishment (LFEE) 1833-1865

FOLLOWING the Great Fire of London in 1666, which devastated a large part of London, a disaster that London was not prepared for, measures to prevent such disasters from happening again were put into place. The Common Council of the City in 1668 decided to divide the City into four areas in which hundreds of leather buckets, ladders of various sizes, pick - axe hatchets and shod shovels would be provided. It was in this same year that the first regular fire insurance office was established in London.

By the end of the 17th century, many more Insurance companies had set up Fire Offices, but so many claims had been made against them that the larger companies had decided to provide firemen to protect their insured properties. To distinguish these buildings from the others, wall plaques were fixed to the outside to enable their firemen to only extinguish property insured by them (in some parts of London these plaques can still be seen attached to the outside walls of houses). When firemen arrived at a fire and the plaque was not of their company, they would watch the building burn and obstruct the other firemen when they arrived. Local parishes in London also provided manual fire engines, these were kept at or near to the local churches.

Like those of the other Offices, the Sun's Brigade was retained for most of the 18th century on an entirely independent footing. The number of fire engines maintained during the earlier part of the century and the stations at which they were kept is impossible now to trace but by 1789 there were stations at Ratcliffe Highway, Holborn, Gt Swallow Street, Lincoln's Inn Fields and Hornsey Down – all maintained and repaired by independent contractors. In addition the Office had built two barge engines on the Thames to fight riverside fires. The first of these was ordered in August 1765; two years later a second barge engine was built and both were still in use at the end of the century.

At the same time the Royal Exchange was known to have an engine at the Guildhall and the Phoenix in Well Close Square. The Alliance Assurance kept an engine in Hanover Square and eventually moved it to a shed, erected for £7, in the yard of Trinity Chapel in Conduit Street. The Westminster Office kept an engine at Hungerford Market. In 50 years of the Westminster Office they had 36 fully trained and well equipped firemen with five fire engines of the most up-to-date type available. The Eagle & British Dominions Insurance Company kept an engine that they had acquired in a small old house in Hozier Lane, Smithfield, and another engine house in Fleet Market that was rented for £44 per annum. The firemen of the time were recruited from the watermen of the Thames; they were paid 6d (2½ pence). For a small fire such as a chimney, 1s (5 pence) for a large fire and 2/6d (12½ pence) for a serious fire which would take several hours work.

Early into the 19th century the insurance companies were asked to join their firemen together to form one brigade, but it was not until 1825 that the first of the larger companies decided to join forces. In 1832, on the 20th July, representatives from the Alliance, Atlas, Globe, Imperial, London, Protector, Royal Exchange, Sun, Union and Westminster offices met at the Sun Fire Office at Bank Buildings to consider the formation of a 'General Fire Engine Establishment' for London.

At a following meeting on the 6th August 1832, it was decided to proceed with the formation of the Establishment. It should consist of a Superintendent, 5 foremen, 9 engineers and 66 firemen with 14 engines one floating engine and 5 spare engines. The engines suitable for fire stations and staff (not including the Superintendent) would be transferred from the fire brigades of the offices joining the Establishment and the estimated cost of £7,000 per annum would be borne by the member offices in proportion partly to the extent of their business in London and the amount of their present expenses, £400 per annum being the lowest amount that an office would pay. The following companies were also interested in joining, British, County, Guardian, Hand in Hand, Norwich Union, Phoenix & West of England offices; which were maintaining firemen in London at the time and if all of these joined it would provide an extra 8 engines and 40 staff.

On 1st January 1833 the London Fire Engine Establishment was formed. James Braidwood was chosen to be the first superintendent with 76 men and all the equipment from all the companies. During the existence of the Establishment some companies dropped out, most due to amalgamation. The equipment the new Establishment used was improved over the years. At the beginning the land engines were all horse drawn and manually operated and there was one oar-propelled wooden fire float with a manual pump. The fire float was essential for use in dock warehouse fires along the Thames where most of the greater risks were. A new boat arrived in 1837 and another in 1846 which was a iron hulled boat which replaced the earlier float. By 1852 a float was fitted with steam engines to work the pumps and to propel the vessel. The first steam engine for the Establishment was hired from Messrs Shand & Mason in 1860 for £65 for one year. At the end of this period it was purchased outright. Prior to this date Braidwood had declined from using steam engines and kept to manuals, which had been improved over the years.

During 1862 a large steam engine was purchased for £650 and two smaller ones purchased for £350 each from Messrs Shand & Mason. Early on communication between stations was by hand i.e, a runner but by 1863 all the stations were in communication with each other by electric telegraph.

STATIONS OF THE LFEE

RATCLIFFE	Princes Square (closed 12/1835)
ST.MARY AXE	Jeffries Square
FINSBURY	White Cross Street
CHEAPSIDE	Watling Street (no. 68)
	Double station
BLACKFRIARS	Farringdon Street
HOLBORN	French Horn Yard
COVENT GARDEN	Bedfordbury
OXFORD STREET	Wells Street
GOLDEN SQUARE	King Street
PORTMAN SQUARE	King Street corner Baker Street
WATERLOO BRIDGE ROAD	Opposite the Coburg Theatre
SOUTHWARK BRIDGE ROAD	near Union Street
TOOLEY STREET	Morgan's Lane

The following are the stations of the extra engines.

SHADWELL	Schoolhouse Lane
WESTMINSTER	Horseferry Road

LAMBETH   Edward Street, Pedlar's - Acre (closed 1839)
ROTHERHITHE   Broadway (the men at this station also
                                 have the floating engine)
FLOATING ENGINE   Off King's Stairs, Rotherhithe

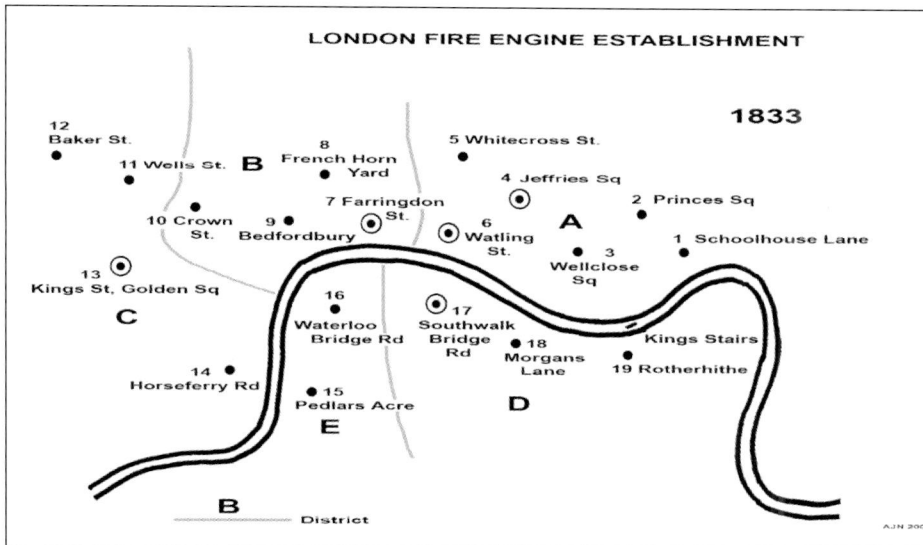

Map of the stations of the London Fire Engine Establishment. c 1833

In 1861 Braidwood tragically died at a serious dockside fire in Tooley Street. The Insurance Companies involved with the LFEE immediately following the fire increased the insurance premiums.

August 1861, the Board of the LFEE met and appointed an Irishman who was the Chief Constable & Chief Officer of the Belfast Fire Brigade, Captain Eyre Massey Shaw to replace Braidwood.

Later the Government asked the committee for the insurance companies to submit a scheme to run a Fire Brigade for the metropolis, Sir George Grey, Home Secretary, in order to satisfy himself with the future cost of a Fire Brigade, requested that Captain Shaw supply an estimate.

By 1864 Captain Shaw set about plans for a Brigade which would cover the Metropolitan Board of Works area, the scheme would go before the Home Secretary then put forward as a bill before Parliament. The following proposals submitted that the cost would amount to the sum of £70,000. The sub-committee of the LFEE in the year 1863 calculated the cost as being £45,000 - £50,000.

Each of the following schemes proposed differ slightly and those amendment are shown in italic in schemes two and three.

SCHEME BY CAPTAIN SHAW FOR A METROPOLITAN FIRE BRIGADE. LONDON FIRE BRIGADE

The following scheme for the protection of the metropolis, within a circle of over twelve miles in diameter, with Charing Cross as a centre, is based on a practical knowledge of the actual condition of London at the present time with regard to risk of fire. The following points being taken into special consideration:-

1.   Population.
2.   Superficial Area.
3.   Nature of Buildings.
4.   Massed Property.
5.   Hazardous Trades.

To meet every contingency, it is obviously most important that the distribution of a Fire Brigade should be widely extended, in order that the first engine, with a skilled fireman, should reach the scene of a fire in the shortest possible time, in comparison with which all other points are of minor importance.

The next matter for careful consideration is the undoubted fact that in this metropolis destructive fires have for the last thirty or forty years taken place, and still continue to take place in close vicinity to Fire Engine Stations, thus proving that even under the most favourable circumstances complete security against fire cannot be obtained in the existing conditions of London.

While therefore I have the distribution first, as a matter of paramount importance, I consider it absolutely necessary, and secondary only to the distribution to provide the means of massing together a large and powerful force at any given spot in the shortest possible time.

In order to carry out effectively both these objects at the same time with the same force, and therefore in the most economical manner, I propose to divide London into six districts, each to be provided with a force of properly trained firemen under the charge of a Foreman or district Engineer, the whole being under the command of one officer, to be styled Chief of the London Fire Brigade.

Each Foreman's district should contain a sufficient number of large stations, in which the fireman should reside, and each large station would have attached to it one or more auxiliary stations, to which men would go on duty by turns for twelve hours at a time.

I consider it desirable to provide four different classes of Fire Engines:-

1. Floating Steam delivering about 4,000 gallons of water per minute.
2. Large Land Steam delivering about 500 gallons of water per minute.
3. Small Land Steam delivering about 200 gallons of water per minute.
4. Under six inch cylinder manual worked by four men, and delivering about twenty gallons per minute.

For the first three classes the same sized hose and other gear at present in use would suffice, and the arrangement for the drawing to fires, &c., would also be somewhat the same, but I think the engines under six inches should be made almost as light as wheelbarrows, and should be provided with canvas hose and coupling screws, with a waterway not exceeding one inch and a half, the whole of the gear being of corresponding lightness, so that one man would be able not only to run this class of engine to a fire at a rate of six or seven miles an hour for the short distance he would have to go, but he could on arrival get to work by himself without waiting for further assistance than what is required and always forthcoming for driving the pumps.

The Foreman of each district should reside in the central station of his command, and the Chief should reside in the central station of the whole, and these centres should be calculated, not geographically alone, but on the basis of five important points already mentioned.

Each Foreman's station should be connected by Alphabetical Telegraph, with every large station in his district, and also with the principal station occupied by the Chief, and each large station should be connected with its own auxiliaries by bell telegraph with about six different sounds.

The proposed London Fire Brigade would consist of 1 Chief and 574 officers and firemen, 4 steam floating fire engines, 6 large land steamers, 66 small land steamers, 154 small manual engines, with horses, drivers, &c., distributed among 54 large and 103 small fire engine stations, and extending over an area of about 120 square miles.

This organization I believe to be the most sound and effective for the present conditions of London, and it is decidedly economical as compared with Fire Brigades either in Europe or America, the total cost being only £70,000 a year for efficiently protecting property valued at £900,000,000 sterling from the ravages of fire.

It is also capable at a trifling expense of being sufficiently modified from time to time to suit the changing requirements of trade and the varying exigencies of the metropolis generally.

In order to be more brief and intelligible, I omit here all details of duties, disciplines, instructions, &c., but I append a series of tables giving full particulars of the original cost and annual expense of every article necessary for the service of an efficient London Fire Brigade with salaries of officers, wages of engineers and firemen, charge for drawing engines to fires &c.

December 5th 1864

Eyre M. Shaw.
Superintendent,
London Fire Engine Establishment.

No. of Stations	No. of Auxiliary Stations	Stations	Rent	Foremen	Engineers	Sub-Engineers	Senior Firemen	Junior Firemen	Totals	Wages
		DISTRICT A	£							£
1	-	Westminster	655	2	2	2	17	17	40	2,660
-	1a	Wood Street, Millbank	30	-	-	-	-	-	-	-
-	1b	Birdcage Walk	30	-	-	-	-	-	-	-
-	1c	Piccadilly	30	-	-	-	-	-	-	-
2	-	Baker Street	330	1	1	1	7	7	17	1,120
-	2a	Marylebone Road	30	-	-	-	-	-	-	-
3	-	Horseferry Road	135	-	1	-	4	5	10	699
-	3a	Millbank Penitentiary	30	-	-	-	-	-	-	-
-	3b	Belgrave Road	30	-	-	-	-	-	-	-
4	-	Buckingham Palace	135	-	1	-	5	6	12	840
-	4a	Chelsea Hospital	30	-	-	-	-	-	-	-
-	4b	Sloane Square	30	-	-	-	5	-	-	834
-	4c	Sloane Street	30	-	-	-	-	-	-	-
5	-	King's Road, Chelsea	135	-	1	-	4	5	10	-
-	5a	King's Road, Chelsea	30	-	-	-	-	-	-	969
-	5b	Cremorne	30	-	-	-	-	-	-	-
6	-	Brompton	135	-	-	-	4	5	10	-
-	6a	Brompton Lane	30	-	-	-	-	-	-	-
-	6b	Gloucester Road	30	-	-	-	-	-	-	834
7	-	Fulham	80	-	-	1	4	5	10	-
-	7a	Walham Green	30	-	-	-	-	-	-	-
-	7b	Parson's Green	30	-	-	-	-	-	-	834
8	-	Hammersmith	80	-	-	1	4	5	-	-
-	8a	North End, Hammersmith	30	-	-	-	-	-	-	-

Stations	Large Steam	Small Steam	Manual under 6"	Total	Repairs	Drivers	Horses	Drawings
DISTRICT A					£			£
Westminster	1	3	2	6	86	2	6	400
Wood Street, Millbank	-	-	1	1	3	-	-	-
Birdcage Walk	-	-	1	1	3	-	-	-
Piccadilly	-	-	1	1	3	-	-	-
Baker Street	-	2	2	4	46	1	4	300
Marylebone Road	-	-	1	1	3	-	-	-
Horseferry Road	-	1	2	2	23	1	2	150
Millbank Penitentiary	-	-	1	1	3	-	-	-
Belgrave Road	-	-	1	1	3	-	-	-
Buckingham Palace	-	1	1	2	23	1	2	150
Chelsea Hospital	-	-	1	1	3	-	-	-
Sloane Square	-	1	1	2	23	1	2	152
Sloane Street	-	-	1	1	3	-	-	-
King's Road, Chelsea	-	-	1	1	3	-	-	-
King's Road, Chelsea	-	1	1	2	23	1	2	150
Cremorne	-	-	1	1	3	-	-	-
Brompton	-	-	1	1	3	-	-	-
Brompton Lane	-	-	1	1	3	-	-	-
Gloucester Road	-	1	1	2	23	1	2	150
Fulham	-	-	1	1	3	-	-	-
Walham Green	-	-	1	1	3	-	-	-
Parson's Green	-	1	1	2	23	1	2	150
Hammersmith	-	-	1	1	3	-	-	-
North End, Hammersmith	-	-	1	1	3	-	-	-

No. of Stations	No. of Auxiliary Stations	Stations	Rent	Foremen	Engineers	Sub-Engineers	Senior Firemen	Junior Firemen	Totals	Wages
		DISTRICT A	£							£
-	8b	Albion Road, Hammersmith	30	-	-	-	-	-	-	-
9	-	Notting Hill	80	-	-	1	4	5	10	700
-	9a	Royal Cresnt, Sheperd's Bush	30	-	-	-	-	-	-	-
-	9b	Ludbury Rd, Westbourne Grove	30	-	-	-	-	-	-	-
10	-	St John's Wood	80	-	-	1	4	5	10	700
-	10a	Wellington Road, St John's Wood	30	-	-	-	-	-	-	-
-	10b	Westbourne Terrace, North	30	-	-	-	-	-	-	-
10	**21**	**TOTALS**	**2,445**	**3**	**7**	**7**	**57**	**65**	**139**	**9,520**
		DISTRICT B								
11	-	Holburn	330	1	1	1	7	7	17	1,120
-	11a	Gray's Inn Lane	30	-	-	-	-	-	-	-
-	11b	Russell Square	30	-	-	-	-	-	-	-
-	11c	Caledonian Road	30	-	-	-	-	-	-	-
12	-	Farrington Street	330	-	1	1	7	7	16	1,120
-	12a	Temple Bar	30	-	-	-	-	-	-	-
13	-	Chandos Street	330	-	1	1	7	7	16	1,120
-	13a	Wellington Street, Strand	30	-	-	-	-	-	-	-
14	-	King Street	135	-	1	-	3	4	8	560
	14a	Great Portland St	30	-	-	-	-	-	-	-
15	-	Crown St, Tottenham Court Rd	135	-	1	-	3	4	8	560
-	15a	Quadrant	30	-	-	-	-	-	-	-
16	-	Hampstead	80	-	-	1	3	4	8	560
-	16a	Avenue Road, Hampstead	30	-	-	-	-	-	-	-
17	-	Camden Town	135	-	1	-	4	5	10	700

Stations	Large Steam	Small Steam	Manual under 6"	Total	Repairs	Drivers	Horses	Drawings
DISTRICT A					£			£
Albion Road, Hammersmith	-	-	1	1	3	-	-	-
Notting Hill	-	1	1	2	23	1	2	100
Royal Cresnt, Shepherd's Bush	-	-	1	1	3	-	-	-
Ludbury Rd, Westbourne Grove	-	-	1	1	3	-	-	-
St John's Wood	-	1	1	2	23	1	2	100
Wellington Road, St John's Wood	-	-	1	1	3	-	-	-
Westbourne Terrace, North	-	-	1	1	3	-	-	-
TOTALS	**1**	**13**	**32**	**46**	**376**	**11**	**26**	**1,700**
DISTRICT B								
Holburn	1	3	1	5	83	1	4	300
Gray's Inn Lane	-	-	1	1	3	-	-	-
Russell Square	-	-	1	1	3	-	-	-
Caledonian Road	-	-	1	1	3	-	-	-
Farrington Street	-	1	1	2	23	1	4	300
Temple Bar	-	-	1	1	3	-	-	-
Chandos Street	-	1	1	2	23	1	4	300
Wellington Street, Strand	-	-	1	1	3	-	-	-
King Street	-	2	1	3	43	1	2	150
Great Portland St	-	-	1	1	3	-	-	-
Crown St, Tottenham Court Rd	-	1	1	2	23	1	2	150
Quadrant	-	-	1	1	3	-	-	-
Hampstead	-	1	1	2	23	1	2	150
Avenue Road, Hampstead	-	-	1	1	3	-	-	-
Camden Town	-	1	1	2	23	1	2	150

No. of Stations	No. of Auxiliary Stations	Stations	Rent	Foremen	Engineers	Sub-Engineers	Senior Firemen	Junior Firemen	Totals	Wages
		DISTRICT B	£							£
-	17a	Euston Square	30	-	-	-	-	-	-	-
-	17b	Hampsted Road	30	-	-	-	-	-	-	-
18	-	Kentish Town	80	-	-	1	3	4	8	560
-	18a	Highgate Rise	30	-	-	-	-	-	-	-
19	-	Highgate	80	-	-	1	3	4	8	560
-	19a	Junction Rd, Upp Holloway	30	-	-	-	-	-	-	-
9	12	**TOTALS**	1,995	1	6	6	40	46	99	6,360
		DISTRICT C								
20	-	Whitecross Street	135	1	1	1	5	5	13	840
-	20a	City Road	30	-	-	-	-	-	-	-
-	20b	Worship Street	20	-	-	-	-	-	-	-
-	20c	Charter House Sq	30	-	-	-	-	-	-	-
21	-	Stoke Newington	80	-	-	1	3	4	8	560
-	21a	Newington Green	30	-	-	-	-	-	-	-
22	-	Kingsland	80	-	-	1	3	4	8	560
-	22a	Downham Road	30	-	-	-	-	-	-	-
23	-	Shoreditch	135	-	1	-	4	5	10	700
-	23a	Kingsland Road	30	-	-	-	-	-	-	-
-	23b	New North Road	30	-	-	-	-	-	-	-
24	-	Watling Street	330	-	1	1	5	5	12	840
-	24a	Moorgate Road	30	-	-	-	-	-	-	-
-	24b	King William Street, City	30	-	-	-	-	-	-	-
-	24c	St. Paul's Churchyard	30	-	-	-	-	-	-	-
25	-	Islington	330	-	1	1	5	5	12	840

Stations	Large Steam	Small Steam	Manual under 6"	Total	Repairs	Drivers	Horses	Drawings
DISTRICT B					£			£
Euston Square	-	-	1	1	3	-	-	-
Hampsted Road	-	-	1	1	3	-	-	-
Kentish Town	-	1	1	2	23	1	2	100
Highgate Rise	-	-	1	1	3	-	-	-
Highgate	-	1	1	23	3	1	2	100
Junction Rd, Upp Holloway	-	-	1	1	3	-	-	-
TOTALS	**1**	**12**	**21**	**34**	**323**	**9**	**24**	**1,650**
DISTRICT C								
Whitecross Street	-	2	1	3	43	1	2	150
City Road	-	-	1	1	3	-	-	-
Worship Street	-	-	1	1	3	-	-	-
Charter House Sq	-	-	1	1	3	-	-	-
Stoke Newington	-	1	1	2	23	1	2	100
Newington Green	-	-	1	1	3	-	-	-
Kingsland	-	1	1	2	23	1	2	100
Downham Road	-	-	1	1	3	-	-	-
Shoreditch	-	2	1	3	43	1	2	150
Kingsland Road	-	-	1	1	3	-	-	-
New North Road	-	-	1	1	3	-	-	-
Watling Street	1	2	1	4	63	1	4	300
Moorgate Road	-	-	1	1	3	-	-	-
King William Street, City	-	-	1	1	3	-	-	-
St. Paul's Churchyard	-	-	1	1	3	-	-	-
Islington	-	2	1	1	43	1	4	300

No. of Stations	No. of Auxiliary Stations	Stations	Rent	Foremen	Engineers	Sub-Engineers	Senior Firemen	Junior Firemen	Totals	Wages
		DISTRICT C	£							£
-	25a	Lower Road, Islington	30	-	-	-	-	-	-	-
-	25b	St John's Street	30	-	-	-	-	-	-	-
-	25c	Richmond Rd, Calendonian Rd	30	-	-	-	-	-	-	-
26	-	Holloway	80	-	-	1	4	5	10	700
-	26a	Seven Sisters' Road	30	-	-	-	-	-	-	-
-	26b	Highbury Cresent	30	-	-	-	-	-	-	-
7	**15**	**TOTALS**	**1,620**	**1**	**4**	**6**	**29**	**33**	**73**	**5,040**
		DISTRICT D								
27	-	Wellclose Square	330	1	1	1	8	8	19	840
-	27a	High Street, Shadwell	30	-	-	-	-	-	-	-
-	27b	Wapping	30	-	-	-	-	-	-	-
-	27c	East Smithfield	30	-	-	-	-	-	-	-
28	-	Hackney Church	80	-	-	1	5	6	12	840
-	28a	Hackney Wick	30	-	-	-	-	-	-	-
-	28b	Richmond Rd, Hackney	30	-	-	-	-	-	-	-
-	28c	Upper Clapton	30	-	-	-	-	-	-	-
29	-	Bethnal Green	135	-	1	-	4	5	10	700
-	29a	Mare Street, Hackney	30	-	-	-	-	-	-	-
-	29b	Bethnal Green Road	30	-	-	-	-	-	-	-
30	-	Mile End	135	-	1	1	5	5	10	840
-	30a	Grove Road, Mile End	30	-	-	-	-	-	-	-
-	30b	Cambridge Road, Mile End	30	-	-	-	-	-	-	-
-	30c	Bethnal Green	30	-	-	-	-	-	-	-
31	-	Bow	80	-	-	1	4	5	10	700

Stations	Large Steam	Small Steam	Manual under 6"	Total	Repairs	Drivers	Horses	Drawings
DISTRICT C					£			£
Lower Road, Islington	-	-	1	1	3	-	-	-
St John's Street	-	-	1	1	3	-	-	-
Richmond Rd, Calendonian Rd	-	-	1	1	3	-	-	-
Holloway	-	1	1	2	23	1	2	100
Seven Sisters' Road	-	-	1	1	3	-	-	-
Highbury Cresent	-	-	1	1	3	-	-	-
TOTALS	**1**	**11**	**22**	**34**	**306**	**7**	**18**	**1,200**
DISTRICT D								
Wellclose Square	1	2	1	4	63	1	4	300
High Street, Shadwell	-	-	1	1	3	-	-	-
Wapping	-	-	1	1	3	-	-	-
East Smithfield	-	-	1	1	3	-	-	-
Hackney Church	-	1	1	2	23	1	2	100
Hackney Wick	-	-	1	1	3	-	-	-
Richmond Rd, Hackney	-	-	1	1	3	-	-	-
Upper Clapton	-	-	1	1	3	-	-	-
Bethnal Green	-	1	1	2	23	1	2	150
Mare Street, Hackney	-	-	1	1	3	-	-	-
Bethnal Green Road	-	-	-	-	-	-	-	-
Mile End	-	1	1	2	23	1	2	150
Grove Road, Mile End	-	-	1	1	3	-	-	-
Cambridge Road, Mile End	-	-	1	1	3	-	-	-
Bethnal Green	-	-	1	1	3	-	-	-
Bow	-	1	1	2	23	1	2	100

No. of Stations	No. of Auxiliary Stations	Stations	Rent	Foremen	Engineers	Sub-Engineers	Senior Firemen	Junior Firemen	Totals	Wages
		DISTRICT D	£							£
-	31a	Old Ford	30	-	-	-	-	-	-	-
-	31b	Stratford Road	30	-	-	-	-	-	-	-
32	-	Barking Road	135	-	1	-	4	5	10	700
-	32a	East India Dock's	30	-	-	-	-	-	-	-
-	32b	Bromley	30	-	-	-	-	-	-	-
33	-	West India Dock's	135	-	1	-	3	4	8	560
-	33a	West Ferry Rd, Millwall	30	-	-	-	-	-	-	-
34	-	Ratcliff	135	-	1	1	4	5	10	700
-	34a	Narrow Street, Limehouse	30	-	-	-	-	-	-	-
-	34b	Commercial Road	30	-	-	-	-	-	-	-
35	-	Isle of Dogs	80	-	1	-	3	4	8	560
-	35a	Stone Wharf, Isle of Dogs	30	-	-	-	-	-	-	-
36	-	Houndsditch	135	-	1	-	4	5	10	700
-	36a	Brick Lane, Spitalfields	30	-	-	-	-	-	-	-
-	36b	Tower Hill	30	-	-	-	-	-	-	-
10	**21**	**TOTALS**	**2,010**	**1**	**7**	**5**	**41**	**49**	**103**	**7,140**
		DISTRICT E								
37	-	Kent Road	135	1	1	1	5	5	13	840
-	37a	Hatcham	30	-	-	-	-	-	-	-
-	37b	Peckham	30	-	-	-	-	-	-	-
-	37c	Grange Road	30	-	-	-	-	-	-	-
38	-	Rotherhithe	135	-	1	1	5	5	12	840
-	38a	Deptford, Lower Road	30	-	-	-	-	-	-	-
-	38b	Blue Anchor Road	30	-	-	-	-	-	-	-

Stations	Large Steam	Small Steam	Manual under 6"	Total	Repairs	Drivers	Horses	Drawings
DISTRICT D					£			£
Old Ford	-	-	1	1	3	-	-	-
Stratford Road	-	-	1	1	3	-	-	-
Barking Road	-	1	1	2	23	1	2	150
East India Dock's	-	-	1	1	3	-	-	-
Bromley	-	-	1	1	3	-	-	-
West India Dock's	-	1	1	2	23	1	2	150
West Ferry Rd, Millwall	-	-	1	1	3	-	-	-
Ratcliff	-	2	1	3	43	1	2	150
Narrow Street, Limehouse	-	1	1	2	23	1	2	150
Commercial Road	-	-	1	1	3	-	-	-
Isle of Dogs	-	-	1	1	3	-	-	-
Stone Wharf, Isle of Dogs	-	-	1	1	3	-	-	-
Houndsditch	-	1	1	2	23	1	2	150
Brick Lane, Spitalfields	-	-	1	1	3	-	-	-
Tower Hill	-	-	1	1	3	-	-	-
TOTALS	**1**	**12**	**31**	**44**	**353**	**10**	**22**	**1,500**
DISTRICT E								
Kent Road	-	1	1	2	23	1	2	150
Hatcham	-	-	1	1	3	-	-	-
Peckham	-	-	1	1	3	-	-	-
Grange Road	-	-	1	1	3	-	-	-
Rotherhithe	-	1	1	2	23	1	2	150
Deptford, Lower Road	-	-	1	1	3	-	-	-
Blue Anchor Road	-	-	1	1	3	-	-	-

No. of Stations	No. of Auxiliary Stations	Stations	Rent	Foremen	Engineers	Sub-Engineers	Senior Firemen	Junior Firemen	Totals	Wages
		DISTRICT E	£							£
-	38c	Bermondsey Wall	30	-	-	-	-	-	-	-
39	-	Deptford	135	-	1	1	5	5	12	840
-	39a	East Country Docks	30	-	-	-	-	-	-	-
-	39b	High Street, Deptford	30	-	-	-	-	-	-	-
-	39c	Commercial Docks	30	-	-	-	-	-	-	-
40	-	Greenwich	135	-	1	1	5	5	12	840
-	40a	Trafalgar Rd, Greenwich	30	-	-	-	-	-	-	-
-	40b	Blackheath Hill	30	-	-	-	-	-	-	-
-	40c	Deptford Bridge	30	-	-	-	-	-	-	-
41	-	Lewisham	80	-	-	1	4	5	10	700
-	41a	Blackheath	30	-	-	-	-	-	-	-
-	41b	Lee	30	-	-	-	-	-	-	-
42	-	Dulwich	80	-	-	1	4	5	10	700
-	42a	Peckham Rye	30	-	-	-	-	-	-	-
-	42b	Herne Hill	30	-	-	-	-	-	-	-
43	-	Southwark Bridge Road	135	-	1	1	5	5	12	840
-	43a	Wellington St, London Br	30	-	-	-	-	-	-	-
-	43b	Great Dover Street	30	-	-	-	-	-	-	-
-	43c	Charlotte St, Blackfriars Rd	30	-	-	-	-	-	-	-
44	-	Tooley Street	330	-	1	1	5	5	12	840
-	44a	Dockhead	30	-	-	-	-	-	-	-
-	44b	Long Lane, Bermondsey	30	-	-	-	-	-	-	-
8	**21**	**TOTALS**	**1,795**	**1**	**6**	**8**	**38**	**40**	**93**	**6,440**

Stations	Large Steam	Small Steam	Manual under 6"	Total	Repairs	Drivers	Horses	Drawings
DISTRICT E					£			£
Bermondsey Wall	-	-	1	1	3	-	-	-
Deptford	-	1	1	2	23	1	2	150
East Country Docks	-	-	1	1	3	-	-	-
High Street, Deptford	-	-	1	1	3	-	-	-
Commercial Docks	-	-	1	1	3	-	-	-
Greenwich	-	1	1	2	23	1	2	150
Trafalgar Rd, Greenwich	-	-	1	1	3	-	-	-
Blackheath Hill	-	-	1	1	3	-	-	-
Deptford Bridge	-	-	1	1	3	-	-	-
Lewisham	-	1	1	2	23	1	2	100
Blackheath	-	-	1	1	3	-	-	-
Lee	-	-	1	1	3	-	-	-
Dulwich	-	1	1	2	23	1	2	100
Peckham Rye	-	-	1	1	3	-	-	-
Herne Hill	-	-	1	1	3	-	-	-
Southwark Bridge Road	1	2	1	4	63	1	2	150
Wellington St, London Br	-	-	1	1	3	-	-	-
Great Dover Street	-	-	1	1	3	-	-	-
Charlotte St, Blackfriars Rd	-	-	1	1	3	-	-	-
Tooley Street	-	2	1	3	43	1	4	300
Dockhead	-	-	1	1	3	-	-	-
Long Lane, Bermondsey	-	-	1	1	3	-	-	-
TOTALS	1	10	29	40	307	8	18	1,250

No. of Stations	No. of Auxiliary Stations	Stations	Rent	Foremen	Engineers	Sub-Engineers	Senior Firemen	Junior Firemen	Totals	Wages
		DISTRICT F								
45	-	Kennington Oval	135	1	1	1	6	6	15	980
-	45a	Walcot Place	30	-	-	-	-	-	-	-
-	45b	New Camberwell Rd	30	-	-	-	-	-	-	-
-	45c	North Brixton	30	-	-	-	-	-	-	-
-	45d	Wandsworth Road	30	-	-	-	-	-	-	-
46	-	Waterloo Road	330	-	1	1	5	5	12	840
-	46a	Upper Stamford St	30	-	-	-	-	-	-	-
-	46b	Westminster Road	30	-	-	-	-	-	-	-
-	46c	Bridge Road, Lambeth	30	-	-	-	-	-	-	-
47	-	Walworth, Newington	330	-	1	1	5	5	12	840
-	47a	Camberwell Road	30	-	-	-	-	-	-	-
48	-	Camberwell	80	-	-	1	3	4	8	560
-	48a	Camberwell Lane	30	-	-	-	-	-	-	-
49	-	Clapham	80	-	-	1	4	5	10	700
-	49a	Brixton Causeway	30	-	-	-	-	-	-	-
-	49b	Crescent Rd, Clapham	30	-	-	-	-	-	-	-
50	-	Wandsworth	80	-	-	1	4	5	10	700
-	50a	Battersea Rise	30	-	-	-	-	-	-	-
-	50b	Putney	30	-	-	-	-	-	-	-
6	**13**	**TOTALS**	**1,425**	**1**	**3**	**6**	**27**	**30**	**67**	**4,620**
		FLOATS								
51	-	Westminster Bridge	-	-	-	-	-	-	-	-
52	-	Southwark Bridge	-	-	-	-	-	-	-	-
53	-	Rotherhithe	-	-	-	-	-	-	-	-

Stations	Large Steam	Small Steam	Manual under 6"	Total	Repairs	Drivers	Horses	Drawings
DISTRICT F								
Kennington Oval	-	1	1	2	23	1	2	150
Walcot Place	-	-	1	1	3	-	-	-
New Camberwell Rd	-	-	1	1	3	-	-	-
North Brixton	-	-	1	1	3	-	-	-
Wandsworth Road	-	-	1	1	3	-	-	-
Waterloo Road	-	2	1	3	43	1	4	300
Upper Stamford St	-	-	1	1	3	-	-	-
Westminster Road	-	-	1	1	3	-	-	-
Bridge Road, Lambeth	-	-	1	1	3	-	-	-
Walworth, Newington	1	2	1	4	63	1	4	300
Camberwell Road	-	-	1	1	3	-	-	-
Camberwell	-	1	1	2	23	1	2	100
Camberwell Lane	-	-	1	1	3	-	-	-
Clapham	-	1	1	2	2	1	2	100
Brixton Causeway	-	-	1	1	3	-	-	-
Crescent Rd, Clapham	-	-	1	1	3	-	-	-
Wandsworth	-	1	1	2	23	1	2	100
Battersea Rise	-	-	1	1	3	-	-	-
Putney	-	-	1	1	3	-	-	-
TOTALS	**1**	**8**	**19**	**28**	**237**	**6**	**16**	**1,050**
FLOATS								
Westminster Bridge	-	-	-	-	100	-	-	-
Southwark Bridge	-	-	-	-	100	-	-	-
Rotherhithe	-	-	-	-	100	-	-	-

No. of Stations	No. of Auxiliary Stations	Stations	Rent	Foremen	Engineers	Sub-Engineers	Senior Firemen	Junior Firemen	Totals	Wages
		FLOATS								
54	-	Limeklin Dock	-	-	-	-	-	-	-	-
		TOTALS								

Stations	Large Steam	Small Steam	Manual under 6"	Total	Repairs	Drivers	Horses	Drawings
FLOATS								
Limeklin Dock	-	-	-	-	100	-	-	-
TOTALS					**400**			

Estimate of first cost of establishing brigade.

Fitting up 50 large stations		@£100	£5,000	
Fitting up 103 small stations		@£20	£2,060	
		Total		**£7,060**

Fire engines,

.. ..	4 floating	@£3,000	£12,000	
.. ..	6 large land steamers	@£800	£4,800	
.. ..	66 small land steamers	@£380	£24,280	
.. ..	154 small manual under 6 inches	@£30	£4,620	
		Total		**£45,700**

Hose & other gear for,

.. ..	4 floats	@£1,000	£4,000	
.. ..	4 hose reels	@£250	£1,000	
.. ..	72 land steamers	@£100	£7,200	
.. ..	154 small manual engines	@£30	£4,620	
		Total		**£16,820**

Telegraph, say	£6,000	
Sundries, including architects, consultant engineer lawyers, Surveyors, negotiators, &c.,	£4,420	
	£10,420	
Total		**£80,000**

Deduct:- Probable saving on purchasing partly used engines and other gear from the present London Fire Engine Establishment and several of the parishes, about £12,000.

Leaving the balance of (as the first cost of establishing the new brigade) about £65,000.

(signed) Eyre M. Shaw, Superintendent.
London Fire Engine Establishment., December 5th 1864

SUMMARY

District		A	B	C	D	E	F	River	Totals
Stations	Large	10	9	7	10	8	6	...	54
	Small	21	12	5	21	21	13	...	103
Rent*		£2,475	£1,995	£1,620	£2,010	£1,796	£1,425	...	£11,320
Men	Foremen	3	1	1	1	1	1	...	8
	Engineers	7	6	4	7	6	3	...	33
	Sub – Engineers	7	6	6	5	8	6	...	38
	Senior Firemen	57	40	29	41	38	27	...	232
	Junior Firemen	65	46	33	49	40	30	...	263
	Totals	139	99	73	103	93	67	...	574
Wages**		£9,520	£6,360	£5,040	£7,140	£6,440	£4,620	...	£39,120
Engines Steam	Floating	...	...	...	...	...	...	4	4
	Large Land	1	1		1	1	1	...	6
	Small Land	13	12	11	12	10	8	...	66
Engines Manual	Under 6in	32	21	22	31	29	10	...	154
	Total	46	34	34	44	10	28	4	330
Coals		...	...	...	£500	...	...	£1,000	£1,500
Repairs***		£376	£323	£306	£353	£307	£237	£400	£2,302
Drivers		11	9	7	10	8	6	...	51
Horses		26	24	18	22	18	16	...	124
Drawings****		£1,700	£1,650	£1,200	£1,500	£1,250	£1,050	...	£8,350

1.	Rent*	£11,320		8.	Turncocks	£300
2.	Salaries	£2,200		9.	Assistants	£1,000
3.	Wages**	£39,120		10.	Refreshments	£1,000
4.	Repairs	£2,302		11.	Drawings****	£8,350
5.	Renewal of stock***	£1,500		12.	Telegraph	£500
6.	Coals	£1,500		13.	Sundries	£708
7.	calls	£200			totals	£70,000

*   Under the head of Rent, are included rent, rates, taxes, gas, painting & repairs.

**   Under the head of Wages, are included wages as at present, clothing @ £7.10s per man and surgeon @ £1 per man.

***   Under the head of repairs to Engines and renewal of Stock combined, are included repairs to hose and small gear generally.

****   Under the head of Drawings, are included horses, drivers and damage from accidents.

December 5th 1864.
(signed) Eyre Massey Shaw, Superintendent.
London fire Engine Establishment.

Mr Waddington to Mr Browne.
Whitehall,
December 9th 1864.

Sir,

I am directed by Secretary Sir George Grey to acquaint you, for the information of the Committee of Representatives of the Fire Insurance Companies, contributing to the London Fire Engine Establishment, that he has under his consideration the former correspondence respecting the protection of the metropolis from fire, with the view, if possible, of introducing a Bill upon the subject in the coming session of parliament.

In order to satisfy himself with respect to the future cost of the service, Sir George Grey requested Captain Shaw to furnish him with an estimate, of which a copy is enclosed. It appears from the estimate that the annual cost of the establishment is calculated at £70,000 besides an outlay at first of £65,000. The amount at which the Sub – Committee of the London Fire Engine Establishment in the year 1863 calculated the cost was from £45,000 to £50,000.

As any arrangements upon which legislation is to be founded must depend in great measure upon a rate to be levied in the metropolis, this increase in the estimated expense, if it is necessary, will raise difficulties that may be insuperable. Sir George Grey is unable himself to check the estimate, and will feel obliged by the opinion of the Committee whether it can be reduced. It does not appear at first sight why a service which is now creditably performed for less than £35,000, per annum, including the expenses paid by the parishes, should require double that amount.

If the estimate can be reduced to £50,000, per annum, including interest on the first outlay, Sir George Grey does not apprehend any serious difficulty in a satisfactory settlement of the question.

I am, &c.
(signed) H. WADDINGTON.

Mr Browne to Sir George Grey.
London Fire Engine Establishment, 68 Watling Street.
December 21st, 1864.

Sir,

I am directed by the Committee for managing this establishment to inform you that they have under consideration Mr. Waddington's letter of the 9th instant, addressed to me, respecting the expenditure necessary for forming and carrying on an effective fire brigade for the metropolis, and pointing out a discrepancy between the estimate of Captain Shaw and the amount referred to in the report of the Sub – Committee of this establishment appointed the 29th of June 1863.

In reply, the Committee wish me to observe that as various amounts of expenditure in an arrangement of this kind involve only the question of relative efficiency, the scale to be adopted must, in their opinion, remain for your decision.

As regards the sum of £50,000 per annum alluded to in the report of the Sub – Committee, it will be seen that the amount is assumed, and is not referred to as a calculation by the Committee, but in as much as that amount considerably exceeds that a brigade very far superior to that now in operation might be formed on the basis of that outlay. In the hope of assisting your views on the subject, the Committee have caused a scheme for a very effective brigade at the cost of £50,000 per annum, inclusive of interest on the sum to be raised for outfit, to be prepared by Captain Shaw, who is authorised to submit the same to you. As a matter of course, a brigade as originally suggested by Captain Shaw, based on an annual expenditure of £70,000, would be more completely efficient than that he will now submit. That estimate was prepared by Captain Shaw by the desire of the Committee, in order to afford information to the Home Office, without any limits of expenditure having been prescribed for his guidance.

The Committee wish me to express their readiness to put at your disposal all the information which, by long experience, they have acquired, and to render you any other assistance in their power to secure that any amount you may decide upon expending for a London Fire Brigade may be applied with the greatest possible efficiency.

I am, &c.,
(signed) W.M. Browne, Hon Sec.

Mr Baring, MP., to Mr. Browne.
Whitehall, January 23rd 1865.

Sir,

With reference to your letter of the 21st December last, I am directed by Secretary Sir George Grey to request that you will furnish him with the estimate for the protection of the district within the jurisdiction of the Metropolitan Board of Works from fire for the sum of £50,000 per annum, including interest on any outlay required, which estimate, Sir George Grey understood, would be sent without a further communication from him.

I am, &c.,
(signed) T.G. BARING.

Mr Browne to Mr Baring, MP.
London Fire Engine Establishment, 68 Watling Street.
January 25th 1865.

Sir,

Referring to my communication of 21st ultimo, I now forward, through Captain Shaw, for the information of the Secretary of state for the Home Office Department, his estimate therein alluded to.

I must, however, observe, that the estimate as prepared does not include interest on the sum to be raised for the outfit within the amount of £50,000 per annum; but, upon careful examination, it appears that such a reduction may be re-arranging the smaller stations as will bring the total within that limit, without materially impairing the efficiency of the proposed new brigade.

I am, &c.,
(signed) W.M. Browne, Hon, Sec.

SCHEME BY CAPTAIN SHAW FOR A METROPOLITAN FIRE BRIGADE.
LONDON FIRE BRIGADE

The following scheme for the protection of the metropolis, within a circle of over *nine* miles in diameter, with Charing Cross as a centre, is based on a practical knowledge of the actual condition of London at the present time with regard to risk of fire. The following points being taken into special consideration:-

1.   Population.
2.   Superficial Area.
3.   Nature of Buildings.
4.   Massed Property.
5.   Hazardous Trades.

To meet every contingency, it is obviously most important that the distribution of a Fire Brigade should be widely extended, in order that the first engine, with a skilled fireman, should reach the scene of a fire in the shortest possible time, in comparison with which all other points are of minor importance.

The next matter for careful consideration is the undoubted fact that in this metropolis destructive fires have for the last thirty or forty years taken place, and still continue to take place in close vicinity to Fire Engine Stations, thus proving that even under the most favourable circumstances complete security against fire cannot be obtained in the existing conditions of London.

While therefore I have the distribution first, as a matter of paramount importance, I consider it absolutely necessary, and secondary only to the distribution to provide the means of massing together a large and powerful force at any given spot in the shortest possible time.

In order to carry out effectively both these objects at the same time with the same force, and therefore in the most economical manner, I propose to divide London into *four* districts, each to be provided with a force of properly trained firemen under the charge of a Foreman or district Engineer, the whole being under the command of one officer, to be styled Chief of the London Fire Brigade.

Each Foreman's district should contain a sufficient number of large stations, in which the fireman should reside, and each large station would have attached to it one or more auxiliary stations, to which men would go on duty by turns for twelve hours at a time.

I consider it desirable to provide four different classes of Fire Engines:-

1. Floating Steam delivering about 4,000 gallons of water per minute.
2. Large Land Steam delivering about 500 gallons of water per minute.
3. Small Land Steam delivering about 200 gallons of water per minute.
4. Under six inch cylinder manual worked by four men, and delivering about twenty gallons per minute.

For the first three classes the same sized hose and other gear at present in use would suffice, and the arrangement for the drawing to fires, &c., would also be somewhat the same, but I think the engines under six inches should be made almost as light as wheelbarrows, and should be provided with canvas hose and coupling screws, with a waterway not exceeding one inch and a half, the whole of the gear being of corresponding lightness, so that one man would be able not only to run this class of engine to a fire at a rate of six or seven miles an hour for the short distance he would have to go, but he could on arrival get to work by himself without waiting for further assistance than what is required and always forthcoming for driving the pumps. The Foreman of each district should reside in the central station of his command, and the Chief should reside in the central station of the whole, and these centres should be calculated, not geographically alone, but on the basis of five important points already mentioned. Each Foreman's station should be connected by Alphabetical Telegraph, with every large station in his district, and also with the principal station occupied by the Chief.

The proposed London Fire Brigade would consist of 1 Chief and 416 officers and firemen, 4 steam floating fire engines, 4 large land steamers, 36 small land steamers, 100 small manual engines, with horses, drivers, &c., distributed among 30 large and 65 small fire engine stations, and extending over an area of about 48 square miles.

This organization I believe to be the most sound and effective for the present conditions of London, and it is decidedly economical as compared with Fire Brigades either in Europe or America, the total cost being only *£52,000* a year for efficiently protecting property valued at £900,000,000 sterling from the ravages of fire. It is also capable at a trifling expense of being sufficiently modified from time to time to suit the changing requirements of trade and the varying exigencies of the metropolis generally.

In order to be more brief and intelligible, I omit here all details of duties, disciplines, instructions, &c., but I append a series of tables giving full particulars of the original cost and annual expense of every article necessary for the service of an efficient London Fire Brigade with salaries of officers, wages of engineers and firemen, charge for drawing engines to fires &c.

January 25th, 1865
(signed) Eyre M, Shaw.
Superintendent London Fire Engine Establishment.
Fire Engine Station, Watling Street, E, C.,

No. of Stations	No. of Auxiliary Stations	Stations	Rent	Foremen	Engineers	Sub-Engineers	Senior Firemen	Junior Firemen	Totals	Wages
		DISTRICT A	£							£
1	-	Westminster	600	-	2	2	17	17	38	2,615
-	1a	Wood Street, Millbank	30	-	-	-	-	-	-	-
-	1b	Birdcage Walk	30	-	-	-	-	-	-	-
-	1c	Piccadilly	30	-	-	-	-	-	-	-
2	-	Baker Street	204	1	1	1	7	7	17	1,104
-	2a	Marylebone Road	120	-	-	-	-	-	-	-
3	-	Camden Town	30	-	1	1	4	4	10	699
-	3a	Chalk Farm	30	-	-	-	-	-	-	-
4	-	King Street, Regent St	144	-	1	1	5	5	12	834
-	4a	Regent's Quadrant	30	-	-	-	-	-	-	-
-	4b	Great Portland St	30	-	-	-	-	-	-	-
5	-	Horseferry Road	144	-	1	1	5	5	12	834
-	5a	Millbank Penitentiary	30	-	-	-	-	-	-	-
-	5b	Belgrave Road	30	-	-	-	-	-	-	-
6	-	Buckingham Palace	168	-	1	1	6	6	14	969
-	6a	Chelsea Hospital	30	-	-	-	-	-	-	-
-	6b	Sloane Square	30	-	-	-	-	-	-	-
-	6c	Sloane Street	30	-	-	-	-	-	-	-
7	-	Brompton	144	-	1	1	5	5	12	834
-	7a	Old Brompon Lane	30	-	-	-	-	-	-	-
-	7b	Gloucester Road, Kensington	30	-	-	-	-	-	-	-
8	-	St. John's Wood	144	-	1	1	5	5	12	834
-	8a	Wellington Road, St. John's Wood	30	-	-	-	-	-	-	-
-	8b	Westbourne Terrace Nth.	30	-	-	-	-	-	-	-

Stations	Large Steam	Small Steam	Manual under 6"	Total	Repairs	Drivers	Horses	Drawings
DISTRICT A					£			£
Westminster	1	3	2	6	86	2	6	400
Wood Street, Millbank	-	-	1	1	3	-	-	-
Birdcage Walk	-	-	1	1	3	-	-	-
Piccadilly	-	-	1	1	3	-	-	-
Baker Street	-	2	2	4	46	1	4	250
Marylebone Road	-	-	1	1	3	-	-	-
Camden Town	-	1	2	2	23	1	2	150
Chalk Farm	-	-	1	1	3	-	-	-
King Street, Regent St	-	1	1	2	23	1	2	150
Regent's Quadrant	-	-	1	1	3	-	-	-
Great Portland St	-	-	1	1	3	-	-	-
Horseferry Road	-	1	1	2	23	1	2	152
Millbank Penitentiary	-	-	1	1	3	-	-	-
Belgrave Road	-	-	1	1	3	-	-	-
Buckingham Palace	-	1	1	2	23	1	2	150
Chelsea Hospital	-	-	1	1	3	-	-	-
Sloane Square	-	-	1	1	3	-	-	-
Sloane Street	-	-	1	1	3	-	-	-
Brompton	-	1	1	2	23	1	2	150
Old Brompon Lane	-	-	1	1	3	-	-	-
Gloucester Road, Kensington	-	-	1	1	3	-	-	-
St. John's Wood	-	1	1	2	23	1	2	150
Wellington Road, St. John's Wood	-	-	1	1	3	-	-	-
Westbourne Terrace Nth.	-	-	1	1	3	-	-	-

No. of Stations	No. of Auxiliary Stations	Stations	Rent	Foremen	Engineers	Sub-Engineers	Senior Firemen	Junior Firemen	Totals	Wages
		DISTRICT A	£							£
8	**16**	**TOTALS**	**2,148**	**1**	**9**	**9**	**54**	**54**	**127**	**£8,723**
		DISTRICT B								
9	-	Farringdon Street	204	1	1	1	7	7	17	1,104
-	9a	Temple Bar	30	-	-	-	-	-	-	-
-	9b	St. Paul's Churchyard	30	-	-	-	-	-	-	-
10	-	Islington	168	-	1	1	6	6	14	969
-	10a	Lower Road, Islington	30	-	-	-	-	-	-	-
-	10b	St. John's Street	30	-	-	-	-	-	-	-
-	10c	Richmond Rd, Caledonian Rd	30	-	-	-	-	-	-	-
11	-	Whitecross Street	144	-	1	1	5	5	12	834
-	11a	City Road	30	-	-	-	-	-	-	-
-	11b	Charter House Square	30	-	-	-	-	-	-	-
12	-	Watling Street	144	-	1	1	5	5	12	834
-	12a	Moorgate Street	30	-	-	-	-	-	-	-
-	12b	King William Street, London Br.	30	-	-	-	-	-	-	-
13	-	Chandos Street	120	-	1	1	4	4	10	699
-	13a	Wellington St, Strand	30	-	-	-	-	-	-	-
14	-	Crown St, corner of Tottenham Court Rd.	144	-	1	1	5	5	12	834
-	14a	Euston Road	30	-	-	-	-	-	-	-
-	14b	Russell Square	30	-	-	-	-	-	-	-
15	-	Holborn	144	-	1	1	5	5	12	834
-	15a	Caledonian Road	30	-	-	-	-	-	-	-
-	15b	Gray's Inn Road	30	-	-	-	-	-	-	-
7		**TOTALS**		**1**	**7**	**7**	**37**	**37**	**89**	**6,108**

Stations	Large Steam	Small Steam	Manual under 6"	Total	Repairs	Drivers	Horses	Drawings
DISTRICT A					£			£
TOTALS	**1**	**11**	**26**	**328**	**318**	**9**	**22**	**1,550**
DISTRICT B								
Farringdon Street	1	2	2	5	66	1	4	250
Temple Bar	-	-	1	1	3	-	-	-
St. Paul's Churchyard	-	-	1	1	3	-	-	-
Islington	-	1	1	2	23	1	2	150
Lower Road, Islington	-	-	1	1	3	-	-	-
St. John's Street	-	-	1	1	3	-	-	-
Richmond Rd, Caledonian Rd	-	-	1	1	3	-	-	-
Whitecross Street	-	1	1	2	23	1	2	150
City Road	-	-	1	1	3	-	-	-
Charter House Square	-	-	1	1	3	-	-	-
Watling Street	-	1	1	2	23	1	2	150
Moorgate Street	-	-	1	1	3	-	-	-
King William Street, London Br.	-	-	1	1	3	-	-	-
Chandos Street	-	1	1	1	23	1	2	150
Wellington St, Strand	-	-	1	1	3	-	-	-
Crown St, corner of Tottenham Court Rd.	-	1	1	2	23	1	1	150
Euston Road	-	-	1	1	3	-	-	-
Russell Square	-	-	1	1	3	-	-	-
Holborn	-	1	1	2	23	1	2	150
Caledonian Road	-	-	1	1	3	-	-	-
Gray's Inn Road	-	-	-	1	3	-	-	-
TOTALS	**1**	**8**	**22**	**31**	**246**	**7**	**16**	**1,150**

No. of Stations	No. of Auxiliary Stations	Stations	Rent	Foremen	Engineers	Sub-Engineers	Senior Firemen	Junior Firemen	Totals	Wages
		DISTRICT C	£							£
16	-	Wellclose Square	228	1	1	1	8	8	19	1,240
-	16a	High Street, Shadwell	30	-	-	-	-	-	-	-
-	16b	Wapping	20	-	-	-	-	-	-	-
-	16c	East Smithfield	30	-	-	-	-	-	-	-
17	-	Bethnal Green	144	-	1	1	5	5	12	834
-	17a	Mare Street, Hackney	30	-	-	-	-	-	-	-
-	17b	Church St, Bethnal Grn	30	-	-	-	-	-	-	-
18	-	Mile End	168	-	1	1	6	6	14	969
-	18a	Grove Road, Mile End	30	-	-	-	-	-	-	-
-	18b	Cambridge Road, Mile End	30	-	-	-	-	-	-	-
-	18c	Green St, Bethnal Grn	30	-	-	-	-	-	-	-
19	-	West India Docks	120	-	1	1	4	4	10	699
-	19a	Westferry Road, Millwall	30	-	-	-	-	-	-	-
20	-	Ratcliff	144	-	1	1	5	5	12	834
-	20a	Narrow St, Limehouse	30	-	-	-	-	-	-	-
-	20b	Commercial Road East	30	-	-	-	-	-	-	-
21	-	Bishopsgate	168	-	1	1	6	6	14	969
-	21a	Brick Lane, Spitalfields	30	-	-	-	-	-	-	-
-	21b	Tower Hill	30	-	-	-	-	-	-	-
-	21c	Worship Street	30	-	-	-	-	-	-	-
22	-	Shoreditch	144	-	1	1	5	5	12	834
-	22a	Kingsland Road	30	-	-	-	-	-	-	-
-	22b	New North Road	30	-	-	-	-	-	-	-
7	**16**	**TOTALS**	**1,556**	**1**	**7**	**7**	**39**	**39**	**93**	**6,379**

Stations	Large Steam	Small Steam	Manual under 6"	Total	Repairs	Drivers	Horses	Drawings
DISTRICT C					£			£
Wellclose Square	1	2	2	5	66	1	4	250
High Street, Shadwell	-	-	1	1	3	-	-	-
Wapping	-	-	1	1	3	-	-	-
East Smithfield	-	-	1	1	3	-	-	-
Bethnal Green	-	1	1	2	23	1	2	150
Mare Street, Hackney	-	-	1	1	3	-	-	-
Church St, Bethnal Grn	-	-	1	1	3	-	-	-
Mile End	-	1	1	2	23	1	2	150
Grove Road, Mile End	-	-	1	1	3	-	-	-
Cambridge Road, Mile End	-	-	1	1	3	-	-	-
Green St, Bethnal Grn	-	-	1	1	3	-	-	-
West India Docks	-	1	1	2	23	1	2	150
Westferry Road, Millwall	-	-	1	1	3	-	-	-
Ratcliff	-	1	1	2	23	1	2	150
Narrow St, Limehouse	-	-	1	1	3	-	-	-
Commercial Road East	-	-	1	1	3	-	-	-
Bishopsgate	-	1	1	2	23	1	2	150
Brick Lane, Spitalfields	-	-	1	1	3	-	-	-
Tower Hill	-	-	1	1	3	-	-	-
Worship Street	-	-	1	1	3	-	-	-
Shoreditch	-	1	1	2	23	1	2	150
Kingsland Road	-	-	1	1	3	-	-	-
New North Road	-	-	1	1	3	-	-	-
TOTALS	**1**	**8**	**24**	**33**	**352**	**7**	**16**	**1,150**

No. of Stations	No. of Auxiliary Stations	Stations	Rent	Foremen	Engineers	Sub-Engineers	Senior Firemen	Junior Firemen	Totals	Wages
		DISTRICT D	£							£
23	-	Elephant and Castle	228	1	1	1	8	8	19	1,240
-	23a	Great Dover Street	30	-	-	-	-	-	-	-
-	23b	Camberwell Road	30	-	-	-	-	-	-	-
-	23c	Westminster Road	30	-	-	-	-	-	-	-
24	-	Southwark Bridge Road	144	-	1	1	5	5	12	834
-	24a	Wellington St, London Br.	30	-	-	-	-	-	-	-
-	24b	Charlotte St, Blackfriars Rd	30	-	-	-	-	-	-	-
25	-	Tooley Street	144	-	1	1	5	5	12	834
-	25a	Dockhead	30	-	-	-	-	-	-	-
-	25b	Long Lane, Bermondsey	30	-	-	-	-	-	-	-
26	-	Rotherhithe	168	-	1	1	6	6	14	969
-	26a	Lower Deptford	30	-	-	-	-	-	-	-
-	26b	Ble Anchor Road	30	-	-	-	-	-	-	-
-	26c	Bermondsey Wall	30	-	-	-	-	-	-	-
27	-	Deptford	168	-	1	1	6	6	14	969
-	27a	East Country Docks	30	-	-	-	-	-	-	-
-	27b	Greenwich	30	-	-	-	-	-	-	-
-	27c	Commercial Docks	30	-	-	-	-	-	-	-
28	-	Kent Road	168	-	1	1	6	6	14	969
-	28a	Hatcham	30	-	-	-	-	-	-	-
-	28b	Peckham	30	-	-	-	-	-	-	-
-	28c	Bricklayer's Arms	30	-	-	-	-	-	-	-
29	-	Kennington Oval	120	-	1	1	4	4	10	699
-	29a	Clapham Road	30	-	-	-	-	-	-	-

Stations	Large Steam	Small Steam	Manual under 6"	Total	Repairs	Drivers	Horses	Drawings
DISTRICT D					£			£
Elephant and Castle	1	2	2	5	66	1	4	250
Great Dover Street	-	-	1	1	3	-	-	-
Camberwell Road	-	-	1	1	3	-	-	-
Westminster Road	-	-	1	1	3	-	-	-
Southwark Bridge Road	-	1	1	2	23	1	2	150
Wellington St, London Br.	-	-	1	1	3	-	-	-
Charlotte St, Blackfriars Rd	-	-	1	1	3	-	-	-
Tooley Street	-	1	1	2	23	1	2	150
Dockhead	-	-	1	1	3	-	-	-
Long Lane, Bermondsey	-	-	1	1	3	-	-	-
Rotherhithe	-	1	1	2	23	1	2	150
Lower Deptford	-	-	1	1	3	-	-	-
Ble Anchor Road	-	-	1	1	3	-	-	-
Bermondsey Wall	-	-	1	1	3	-	-	-
Deptford	-	1	1	2	23	1	2	150
East Country Docks	-	-	1	1	3	-	-	-
Greenwich	-	-	1	1	3	-	-	-
Commercial Docks	-	-	1	1	3	-	-	-
Kent Road	-	1	1	2	23	1	2	150
Hatcham	-	-	1	1	3	-	-	-
Peckham	-	-	1	1	3	-	-	-
Bricklayer's Arms	-	-	1	1	3	-	-	-
Kennington Oval	-	1	1	2	23	1	2	150
Clapham Road	-	-	1	1	3	-	-	-

No. of Stations	No. of Auxiliary Stations	Stations	Rent	Foremen	Engineers	Sub-Engineers	Senior Firemen	Junior Firemen	Totals	Wages
		DISTRICT D	£							£
30	-	Waterloo Road	144	-	1	1	5	5	12	834
-	30a	Upper Stamford Streeet	30	-	-	-	-	-	-	-
-	30b	Bridge Road, Lambeth	30	-	-	-	-	-	-	-
8	12	**TOTALS**	1,854	1	8	8	45	45	107	7,348

Stations	Large Steam	Small Steam	Manual under 6"	Total	Repairs	Drivers	Horses	Drawings
DISTRICT D					£			£
Waterloo Road	-	1	1	2	23	1	2	150
Upper Stamford Streeet	-	-	1	1	3	-	-	-
Bridge Road, Lambeth	-	-	1	1	3	-	-	-
TOTALS	**1**	**91**	**28**	**38**	**284**	**8**	**18**	**1,300**

District			A	B	C	D	River	Totals
Stations		Large	8	7	7	8	....	30
		Small	16	14	16	19	....	65
		Rent +a	£2.148	£1.488	£1.596	£1.854	....	£7.086
Men		Foremen	1	1	1	1	....	4
		Engineers	9	7	7	8	....	31
		Sub - Engineers	9	7	7	8	....	31
		Senior Firemen	54	37	39	45	....	175
		Junior Firemen	54	37	39	45	....	175
		Total	127	89	93	107	....	416
		Wages +b	£8.723	£6.108	£6.379	£7.348	....	£28.558
Engines		Steam Floating	....	....	....	....	4	4
		Steam Large Land	1	1	1	1	....	4
		Steam Small Land	11	8	8	9	....	36
		Manual under 6in.	26	22	24	28	....	100
		Total	38	31	33	38	....	140
		Coals	....	....	....	....	£1,000	£1,000
		Repairs +c	£318	£246	£252	£284	£400	£1.500
		Drivers	9	7	7	8	....	31
		Horses	22	16	16	18	....	172
		Drawings +d	£1.550	£1.150	£1.150	£1.300	....	£5.150

1.	Rent	£7.036		9.	Assistance	£1000
2.	Salaries	£1.800		10.	Refreshments	£1000
3.	Wages	£28.558		11.	Drawings	£5.150
4.	Repairs	£1.500		12.	Telegraph	£500
5.	Renewal of stock	£1000		13.	Sundries	£406
6.	Coals	£1.500		14	Interest	£2000
7.	Calls	£200				
8.	Turncocks	£300		Totals		£52.000

+ a   Under the head of Rents are included rent, taxes, gas, painting and repairs.
+ b   Under the head of wages are included wages as at present, clothing at £7 10s per man and surgeon at £1 per man.
+ c   Under the head of Repairs to Engines and Renewal of stock combined, are included repairs to hose and small gear generally.
+ d   Under the head of Drawings are included horses, drivers, and damage from accidents.

REDUCED ESTIMATE OF FIRST COST OF ESTABLISHING BRIGADE.

Fitting up 30 large stations		*@£100*	*£3,000*
Fitting up 65 small stations		*@£20*	*£1,300*
			Total £4,300
Fire engines,			
.. ..	*4 floating*	*@£3,000*	*£12,000*
.. ..	*4 large land steamers*	*@£800*	*£3,200*
.. ..	*36 small land steamers*	*@£380*	*£13,680*

| .. .. | 100 small manual engines | @£30 | £3,000 | |
| | | | Total | £31,880 |

Hose & other gear for,	4 floats	@£1,000	£4,000	
.. ..	4 hose reels	@£250	£1,000	
.. ..	40 land steamers	@£100	£4,000	
.. ..	100 small manual engines	@£30	£3,000	
			Total	£12,000

Telegraph, say			£3,500	
Sundries, including architects, consultant engineer lawyers,			£3,320	
Surveyors, negotiators, &c.,			Total	£6,820
		Total		£55,000

Deduct:- Probable saving on purchasing partly – used engines and other gear from the present London Fire Engine Establishment and several of the parishes, about £15,000.

Leaving the balance of (as the first cost of establishing the new brigade) about £40,000.

COMPARISON OF EFFICIENCY OF THE PROPOSED FIRE BRIGADE WITH THAT OF THE BRIGADE AT PRESENT IN OPERATION.

	Present Brigade	Proposed Brigade	Increase
No. of stations	17	95	78
No. of firemen	131	416	285
Area of which the stations extend in sq.miles	10	48	38
No. of floating steam engines	2	4	2
No. of large land steamers	2	4	2
No. of small land steamers	6	36	30
No. of manual engines	33	100	67
Total no. of engines	43	144	101

January 25th 1865.
(signed) Eyre M. Shaw Superintendent.
London Fire Engine Establishment.
Fire Engine Station, Watling Street, E.C.,

Mr. Baring, MP., to Mr. Browne.
Whitehall, January 27th,
1865

Sir,

I am directed by Secretary Sir George Grey to acknowledge the receipt of your letter of the 35th instant, and to make the following observations:-

The scheme of Captain Shaw for the protection of the metropolis from fire is based upon affording protection to a district embracing 9 miles in diameter from Charing Cross; the area, probably, is nearly equivalent to the district under the Metropolitan Board of Works, but Sir George Grey requests that the scheme may be adapted precisely to that district.

In the estimate of the first cost of establishing the Brigade, provision is made for the purchase of engines, &c., from the present London Fire Engine Establishment; but Sir George Grey presumes that the Committee adhere to the proposal contained in your letter of the 18th April last, that if a satisfactory arrangement is made, "the associated offices will be prepared to transfer the whole of their plant, stock, and staff, with the interest they hold in the stations, subject to the existing liabilities of the establishment, to the new Metropolitan Fire Brigade;" it will be convenient that the nature and amount of the existing liabilities should be stated precisely.

Sir George Grey would be glad that the total estimate should be reduced, including all salaries, expenses, and interest, to sum not exceeding £50,000.

I am also to request that you will inform him if the Associated Offices adhere to their proposal to contribute £35 per £1,000,000 on the sum insured, as explained in their letter of the 21st June last; and it would be convenient if the amount of this contribution, calculated upon the basis of 1863, could be stated.

I am, &c.
(signed) T.E. Baring

Mr. Browne to Mr Baring, MP.
London Fire Engine Establishment, 68 Watling Street,
February 1st, 1865

Sir,

I had the pleasure of laying your favour of the 27th ultimo before the Committee for managing this establishment at their meeting on Monday last. I am requested by them to acquaint you, in reply, for the information of Secretary Sir George Grey, that they are prepared to abide by the offer contained in their previous correspondence, viz., to contribute annually a sum equal to £35 per £1,000,000 on the sum insured towards the new Fire Brigade, and to transfer the whole of their plant, stock, and staff, subject to present liabilities, free of charge, on condition that the existing stations and staff be maintained in the same state of efficiency as they now are; and that the sum to be contributed shall not exceed 30 percent of the amount to be raised for the purpose by a metropolitan rate.

The Committee wish me to draw your attention to the fact that the area of the district under the Metropolitan Board of Works appears, from the information now afforded, greatly to exceed that contemplated by Captain Shaw, in the scheme prepared by him. The Associated fire Insurance Companies are however, prepared to support any scheme for a Fire Brigade which complies with the requirements herein before stated.

I have also to inform you that the amount of contribution by the Associated Insurance Offices calculated on their business of 1863 would amount to £10,156.

A statement of the nature and amount of the existing liabilities of the establishment will be prepared and forwarded to you on a future occasion.

The Committee have also requested that Captain Shaw will furnish secretary Sir George Grey with any suggestions and information he may require on this subject, but always with reference to the before-named conditions.

The Committee are of opinion that there does not exist any sufficient reason for relinquishing, as a source of revenue, the fines proposed by the original Bill prepared by Sir George Grey, to be levied on the owners and occupiers of property where a fire breaks out, all insured property being, in consideration of the sum proposed to be contributed by the Insurance Companies, exempted from the payment of such fines, except for fires occurring in chimneys.

I am &c.
(signed) M. Browne, Hon.Sec.

LONDON FIRE BRIGADE.

The following scheme for the protection of the whole of London and its vicinity, within the District of the Metropolitan board of Works at a cost of £50,000 per annum is based on a practical knowledge of the actual condition of London at the present time with regard to risk of fire.

The following points being taken into special consideration:-

1.   Population
2.   Superficial Area
3.   Nature of Buildings
4.   Massed Property
5.   Hazardous Trades

To meet every contingency, it is obviously most important that the distribution of a Fire Brigade should be widely extended, in order that the first engine, with a skilled fireman, should reach the scene of a fire in the shortest possible time, in comparison with which all other points are of minor importance.

The next matter for careful consideration is the undoubted fact that in this metropolis destructive fires have for the last thirty or forty years taken place, and still continue to take place in close vicinity to Fire Engine Stations, thus proving that even under the most favourable circumstances complete security against fire cannot be obtained in the existing conditions of London.

While therefore I have the distribution first, as a matter of paramount importance, I consider it absolutely necessary, and secondary only to the distribution to provide the means of massing together a large and powerful force at any given spot in the shortest possible time.

In order to carry out effectively both these objects at the same time with the same force, and therefore in the most economical manner, I propose to divide London into *four* – districts, each to be provided with a force of properly trained firemen under the charge of a Foreman or district Engineer, the whole being under the command of one officer, to be styled Chief of the London Fire Brigade.

Each Foreman's district should contain a sufficient number of large stations, in which the fireman should reside, and each large station would have attached to it one or more auxiliary stations, to which men would go on duty by turns for twelve hours at a time. For economy several of the outlying stations might be worked by *contract* at a fixed rate.

I consider it desirable to provide *five* different classes of Fire Engines :-

1. Floating Steam delivering about 4,000 gallons of water per minute.
2. Large Land Steam delivering about 500 gallons of water per minute.
3. Small Land Steam delivering about 200 gallons of water per minute.
4. *Manual-engines, to be drawn by horses, some six and seven inch cylinders to be kept at contract stations.*
5. Manual-engines drawn and worked by men, under six inch cylinders, and delivering about twenty gallons per minute.

For the first *four* classes the same sized hose and other gear at present in use would suffice, and the arrangement for the drawing to fires, &c., would also be somewhat the same, but I think the engines under six inches should be made almost as light as wheelbarrows, and should be provided with hose and coupling screws, with a waterway not exceeding one inch and a half, the whole of the gear being of corresponding lightness, so that one man would be able not only to run this class of engine to a fire at a rate of six or seven miles an hour for the short distance he would have to go, but he could on arrival get to work by himself without waiting for further assistance than what is required and always forthcoming for driving the pumps.

The Foreman of each district should reside in the central station of his command, and the Chief should reside in the central station of the whole, and these centres should be calculated, not geographically alone, but on the basis of five important points already mentioned. *For the proper protection of London the central station should be on the waterside, and should be supplied with a floating pier.*

Each Foreman's station should be connected by Alphabetical Telegraph, with every large station in his district, and also with the principal station occupied by the Chief.

The proposed London Fire Brigade would consist of 1 Chief and 350 officers and firemen, 4 steam floating fire engines, 4 large land steamers, 27 small land steamers, 37 large manual engines and 57 small manual engines, with horses, drivers, &c., distributed among 33 large and 56 small fire engine stations, and protecting an area of about 117square miles.

This organization I believe to be the most sound and effective for the present conditions of London, and it is decidedly economical as compared with Fire Brigades either in Europe or America, the total cost being only *£50,000* a year for efficiently protecting property valued at £900,000,000 sterling from the ravages of fire.

It is also capable at a trifling expense of being sufficiently modified from time to time to suit the changing requirements of trade and the varying exigencies of the metropolis generally.

In order to be more brief and intelligible, I omit here all details of duties, disciplines, instructions, &c., but I append a series of tables giving a summary of the outfit necessary for the service of an efficient London Fire Brigade with salaries of officers, wages of engineers and firemen, charge for drawing engines to fires &c.

Eyre M. Shaw.
Superintendent,
London Fire Engine Establishment.
Fire Engine Station, Watling Street, E.C.,

COMPARISON OF EFFICIENCY OF THE PROPOSED FIRE BRIGADE WITH THAT OF THE BRIGADE PRESENT IN OPERATION.

	Present Brigade	Proposed Brigade	Increase
No. of Stations	17	89	72
No. of Firemen	131	350	219
Area over which stations extended in sq miles	about 10	about 100	90
No. of floating steam engines	2	4	2
No. of large land steamers	2	4	2
No. of small land steamers	6	27	21
No. of manual engines	33	94	61
Total no. of engines	43	129	86

No. of large stns	No. of small stns	No. of contract stns	Stations	Rent	Foremen	Engineers	Sub-Engineers	Senior Firemen	Junior Firemen	Contract Men	Totals	Wages
			DISTRICT A	£								£
1	-	-	Westminster	576	-	2	2	16	16	-	36	2,838
-	1a	-	Horseferry	30	-	-	-	-	-	-	-	-
-	1b	-	Piccadilly, St. James' Church	30	-	-	-	-	-	-	-	-
2	-	-	Baker Street	228	1	1	1	8	8	-	19	1,418
-	2a	-	Marylebone Lane	30	-	-	-	-	-	-	-	-
-	2b	-	Marylebone Road	30	-	-	-	-	-	-	-	-
-	-	3	Camden Road	-	-	-	-	-	-	2	2	150
-	-	3a	Chalk Farm, Kentish Town	-	-	-	-	-	-	2	2	150
4	-	-	King St, Regent St	120	-	1	1	4	4	-	10	804
-	4a	-	Great Portland St	30	-	-	-	-	-	-	-	-
5	-	-	Buckingham Palace	144	-	1	1	5	5	-	12	957
-	5a	-	Sloane Square	30	-	-	-	-	-	-	-	-
-	5b	-	Sloane Street	30	-	-	-	-	-	-	-	-
-	-	6	Fulham Road	-	-	-	-	-	-	2	2	150
	-	6a	Battersea Bridge	-	-	-	-	-	-	2	2	150
-	-	6b	South Kensington	-	-	-	-	-	-	2	2	150
-	-	7	Hammersmith	-	-	-	-	-	-	2	2	150
-	-	7a	Shepherd's Bush	-	-	-	-	-	-	2	2	150
-	-	8	Paddington Green	-	-	-	-	-	-	2	2	150
-	-	8a	Royal Oak	-	-	-	-	-	-	2	2	150
-	-	8b	Harrow Road	-	-	-	-	-	-	2	2	150
-	-	9	St. John's Wood Park	-	-	-	-	-	-	2	2	150
-	-	9a	St. John's Wood Road	-	-	-	-	-	-	2	2	150
-	-	9b	Hampstead	-	-	-	-	-	-	2	2	150

Stations	Large Steam	Small Steam	Large manual	Small Manual	Total	Repairs	Drivers	Horses	Drawings	Total Expense
DISTRICT A						£				£
Westminster	1	3	-	2	6	86	2	6	400	3,900
Horseferry	-	-	-	1	1	3	-	-	-	33
Piccadilly, St. James' Church	-	-	-	1	1	3	-	-	-	33
Baker Street	-	2	-	2	4	46	1	4	250	1,942
Marylebone Lane	-	-	-	1	1	3	-	-	-	33
Marylebone Road	-	-	-	1	1	3	-	-	-	33
Camden Road	-	-	1	-	1	10	-	-	-	160
Chalk Farm, Kentish Town	-	-	1	-	1	10	-	-	-	160
King St, Regent St	-	1	-	1	2	23	1	2	150	1,097
Great Portland St	-	-	-	1	1	3	-	-	-	33
Buckingham Palace	-	1	-	1	2	23	1	2	150	1,274
Sloane Square	-	-	-	1	1	3	-	-	-	33
Sloane Street	-	-	-	1	1	3	-	-	-	33
Fulham Road	-	-	1	-	1	10	-	-	-	160
Battersea Bridge	-	-	1	-	1	10	-	-	-	160
South Kensington	-	-	1	-	1	10	-	-	-	160
Hammersmith	-	-	1	-	1	10	-	-	-	160
Shepherd's Bush	-	-	1	-	1	10	-	-	-	160
Paddington Green	-	-	1	-	1	10	-	-	-	160
Royal Oak	-	-	1	-	1	10	-	-	-	160
Harrow Road	-	-	1	-	1	10	-	-	-	160
St. John's Wood Park	-	-	1	-	1	10	-	-	-	160
St. John's Wood Road	-	-	1	-	1	10	-	-	-	160
Hampstead	-	-	1	-	1	10	-	-	-	160

No. of large stns	No. of small stns	No. of contract stns	Stations	Rent	Foremen	Engineers	Sub-Engineers	Senior Firemen	Junior Firemen	Contract Men	Totals	Wages
			DISTRICT A	£								£
4	**7**	**13**	**TOTALS**	**1,278**	**1**	**5**	**5**	**33**	**33**	**26**	**103**	**7,967**
			DISTRICT B									
10	-	-	Farringdon Street	180	1	1	1	6	6	-	15	1,111
-	10a	-	St.Paul's Churchyard	30	-	-	-	-	-	-	-	-
11	-	-	Islington	144	-	1	1	6	6	-	12	957
-	11a	-	Lower Road, Islington	30	-	-	-	-	-	-	-	-
-	11b	-	Richmond Road, Caledonian Rd	30	-	-	-	-	-	-	-	-
12	-	-	Whitecross Street	120	-	1	1	4	4	-	10	804
-	12a	-	City Road	30	-	-	-	-	-	-	-	-
13	-	-	Watling Street	144	-	1	1	5	5	-	12	957
-	13a	-	Moorgate Street	30	-	-	-	-	-	-	-	-
-	13b	-	King William St, London Bridge	30	-	-	-	-	-	-	-	-
14	-	-	Chandos Street	120	-	1	1	4	4	-	10	804
-	14a	-	Temple Bar	30	-	-	-	-	-	-	-	-
15	-	-	Crown St corner of Tottenham Court Rd	120	-	1	1	4	4	-	10	104
-	15a	-	Euston Square	30	-	-	-	-	-	-	-	-
16	-	-	Holburn	144	-	1	1	5	5	-	12	957
-	16a	-	King's Cross	30	-	-	-	-	-	-	-	-
-	16b	-	Exmouth Street, Clerkenwell	30	-	-	-	-	-	-	-	
-	-	17	Holloway Road	-	-	1	1	-	-	2	2	150
-	-	17a	Upper Holoway	-	-	-	-	-	-	2	2	150
7	**10**	**2**	**TOTALS**	**1,272**	**1**	**7**	**7**	**33**	**33**	**4**	**85**	**36,694**
			DISTRICT C									
18	-	-	Wellclose Square	204	1	1	1	7	7	-	17	1,264

Stations	Large Steam	Small Steam	Large manual	Small Manual	Total	Repairs	Drivers	Horses	Drawings	Total Expense
DISTRICT A						£				£
TOTALS	**1**	**7**	**13**	**13**	**34**	**329**	**5**	**14**	**950**	**10,524**
DISTRICT B										
Farringdon Street	1	2	-	2	5	66	1	4	250	1,607
St.Paul's Churchyard	-	-	-	1	1	3	-	-	-	33
Islington	-	1	-	1	2	23	1	2	150	1,274
Lower Road, Islington	-	-	-	1	1	3	-	-	-	33
Richmond Road, Caledonian Rd	-	-	-	1	1	3	-	-	-	33
Whitecross Street	-	1	-	1	2	23	1	2	150	1,097
City Road	-	-	-	1	1	3	-	-	-	33
Watling Street	-	1	-	1	2	23	1	2	150	1,274
Moorgate Street	-	-	-	1	1	3	-	-	-	33
King William St, London Bridge	-	-	-	1	1	3	-	-	-	33
Chandos Street	-	1	-	1	2	23	1	2	150	1,097
Temple Bar	-	-	-	1	1	3	-	-	-	33
Crown St corner of Tottenham Court Rd	-	1	-	1	2	23	1	2	150	1,097
Euston Square	-	-	-	1	1	3	-	-	-	33
Holburn	-	1	-	1	2	23	1	2	150	1,274
King's Cross	-	-	-	1	1	3	-	-	-	33
Exmouth Street, Clerkenwell	-	-	-	1	1	3	-	-	-	33
Holloway Road	-	-	1	-	1	10	-	-	-	160
Upper Holoway	-	-	1	-	1	10	-	-	-	160
TOTALS	**1**	**8**	**2**	**18**	**29**	**254**	**7**	**16**	**1,150**	**9,370**
DISTRICT C										
Wellclose Square	1	2	-	2	5	66	1	4	250	1,784

No. of large stns	No. of small stns	No. of contract stns	Stations	Rent	Foremen	Engineers	Sub-Engineers	Senior Firemen	Junior Firemen	Contract Men	Totals	Wages
			DISTRICT C	£								£
-	18a	-	Old Gravel Lane	30	-	-	-	-	-	-	-	-
-	18b	-	Minories	30	-	-	-	-	-	-	-	-
19	-	-	Hackney Church	96	-	1	1	3	3	-	8	650
-	-	19a	South Hackney	-	-	-	-	-	-	2	2	150
-	-	19b	Hornsey New Town	-	-	-	-	-	-	2	2	150
-	-	19c	Stoke Newington	-	-	-	-	-	-	2	2	150
20	-	-	Mile End	96	-	1	1	3	3	-	8	650
-	-	20a	Bow Church	-	-	-	-	-	-	2	2	150
-	-	20b	Green St, Bethnal Green	-	-	-	-	-	-	2	2	150
-	-	21	Limehouse Church	-	-	-	-	-	-	2	2	150
-	-	21a	Westferry Road, Millwall	-	-	-	-	-	-	2	2	150
22	-	-	Ratcliff	120	-	1	1	4	4	-	10	804
-	22a	-	Mile End, Old Town	30	-	-	-	-	-	-	-	-
23	-	-	Bishopsgate	144	-	1	1	5	5	-	12	957
-	23a	-	Spitalfields	30	-	-	-	-	-	-	-	-
-	23b	-	Whitechapel Church	30	-	-	-	-	-	-	-	-
-	-	24	Shoreditch	-	-	-	-	-	-	2	2	150
-	-	24a	DE Beauvoir Town	-	-	-	-	-	-	2	2	150
-	-	24b	Bethnal Green	-	-	-	-	-	-	2	2	150
5	**5**	**10**	**TOTALS**	**810**	**1**	**5**	**5**	**22**	**22**	**20**	**75**	**5,825**
			DISTRICT D									
25	-	-	Elephant and Castle	204	1	1	1	7	7	-	17	1,264
-	25a	-	Camberwell Road	30	-	-	-	-	-	-	-	-
-	25b	-	Lambeth walk	30	-	-	-	-	-	-	-	-

Stations	Large Steam	Small Steam	Large manual	Small Manual	Total	Repairs	Drivers	Horses	Drawings	Total Expense
DISTRICT C						£				£
Old Gravel Lane	-	-	-	1	1	3	-	-	-	33
Minories	-	-	-	1	1	3	-	-	-	33
Hackney Church	-	1	-	1	2	23	1	2	150	919
South Hackney	-	-	1	-	1	10	-	-	-	160
Hornsey New Town	-	-	1	-	1	10	-	-	-	160
Stoke Newington	-	-	1	-	1	10	-	-	-	160
Mile End	-	1	-	1	2	23	1	2	150	919
Bow Church	-	-	1	-	1	10	-	-	-	160
Green St, Bethnal Green	-	-	1	-	1	10	-	-	-	160
Limehouse Church	-	-	1	-	1	10	-	-	-	160
Westferry Road, Millwall	-	-	1	-	1	10	-	-	-	160
Ratcliff	-	1	-	1	2	23	1	2	150	1097
Mile End, Old Town	-	-	-	1	1	3	-	-	-	33
Bishopsgate	-	1	-	1	2	23	1	2	150	1,274
Spitalfields	-	-	-	1	1	3	-	-	-	33
Whitechapel Church	-	-	-	1	1	3	-	-	-	33
Shoreditch	-	-	1	-	1	10	-	-	-	160
DE Beauvoir Town	-	-	1	-	1	10	-	-	-	160
Bethnal Green	-	-	1	-	1	10	-	-	-	160
TOTALS	**1**	**6**	**10**	**11**	**28**	**273**	**5**	**12**	**850**	**7,758**
DISTRICT D										
Elephant and Castle	1	2	-	2	5	66	1	4	250	1,784
Camberwell Road	-	-	-	1	1	3	-	-	-	33
Lambeth walk	-	-	-	1	1	3	-	-	-	33

No. of large stns	No. of small stns	No. of contract stns	Stations	Rent	Foremen	Engineers	Sub-Engineers	Senior Firemen	Junior Firemen	Contract Men	Totals	Wages
			DISTRICT D	£								£
26	-	-	Southwark Bridge Road	144	-	1	1	5	5	-	12	957
-	26a	-	Wellington St, London Bridge	30	-	-	-	-	-	-	-	-
-	26b	-	Charlotte St, Blackfriars Rd	30	-	-	-	-	-	-	-	-
27	-	-	Tooley Street	144	-	1	1	5	5	-	12	957
-	27a	-	Dockhead	30	-	-	-	-	-	-	-	-
-	27b	-	Bricklayer's Arms	30	-	-	-	-	-	-	-	-
28	-	-	Rotherhithe	144	-	1	1	5	5	-	12	957
-	28a	-	Lower Road, Deptford	30	-	-	-	-	-	-	-	-
-	28b	-	Blue Anchor Road	30	-	-	-	-	-	-	-	-
-	-	29	Woolwich	-	-	-	-	-	-	2	2	150
-	-	29a	Ditto	-	-	-	-	-	-	2	2	150
-	-	30	Greenwich	-	-	-	-	-	-	2	2	150
-	-	30a	Lewisham	-	-	-	-	-	-	2	2	150
-	-	30b	Deptford	-	-	-	-	-	-	2	2	150
-	-	31	Peckham	-	-	-	-	-	-	2	2	150
-	-	31a	Kent Road	-	-	-	-	-	-	2	2	150
-	-	31b	Hatcham	-	-	-	-	-	-	2	2	150
-	-	31c	Forest Hill	-	-	-	-	-	-	2	2	150
-	-	32	Brixton Road	-	-	-	-	-	-	2	2	150
-	-	32a	Brixton	-	-	-	-	-	-	2	2	150
-	-	32b	Wandsworth	-	-	-	-	-	-	2	2	150
33	-	-	Waterloo Road	120	-	1	1	4	4	-	10	804
-	33a	-	Westminster Road	30	-	-	-	-	-	-	-	-
5	**9**	**12**	**TOTALS**	**1,026**	**1**	**5**	**5**	**26**	**26**	**24**	**87**	**6,739**

Stations	Large Steam	Small Steam	Large manual	Small Manual	Total	Repairs	Drivers	Horses	Drawings	Total Expense
DISTRICT D						£				£
Southwark Bridge Road	-	1	-	1	2	23	1	2	150	1,273
Wellington St, London Bridge	-	-	-	1	1	3	-	-	-	33
Charlotte St, Blackfriars Rd	-	-	-	1	1	3	-	-	-	33
Tooley Street	-	1	-	1	2	23	1	2	150	1,274
Dockhead	-	-	-	1	1	3	-	-	-	33
Bricklayer's Arms	-	-	-	1	1	3	-	-	-	33
Rotherhithe	-	1	-	1	1	23	1	2	150	1,273
Lower Road, Deptford	-	-	-	1	1	3	-	-	-	160
Blue Anchor Road	-	-	-	1	1	3	-	-	-	160
Woolwich	-	-	1	-	1	10	-	-	-	160
Ditto	-	-	1	-	1	10	-	-	-	160
Greenwich	-	-	1	-	1	10	-	-	-	160
Lewisham	-	-	1	-	1	10	-	-	-	160
Deptford	-	-	1	-	1	10	-	-	-	160
Peckham	-	-	1	-	1	10	-	-	-	160
Kent Road	-	-	1	-	1	10	-	-	-	160
Hatcham	-	-	1	-	1	10	-	-	-	160
Forest Hill	-	-	1	-	1	10	-	-	-	160
Brixton Road	-	-	1	-	1	10	-	-	-	160
Brixton	-	-	1	-	1	10	-	-	-	160
Wandsworth	-	-	1	-	1	10	-	-	-	160
Waterloo Road	-	1	-	1	2	23	1	2	150	1,097
Westminster Road	-	-	-	-	1	3	-	-	-	33
TOTALS	**1**	**6**	**12**	**15**	**34**	**305**	**5**	**12**	**850**	**8,920**

District		A	B	C	D	River	Total
Stations	Large	4	7	5	5	...	21
	Small	7	10	5	9	...	31
	Contract	13	2	10	12	...	37
	Rent +1	£1.278	£1.272	£810	£1.026	...	£4.386
Men	Foremen	1	1	1	1	1	5
	Engineers	5	7	5	5	...	22
	Sub - Engineers	5	7	5	5	...	22
	Senior Firemen	33	33	22	26	...	114
	Junior Firemen	33	33	22	26	...	114
	Contract Men	26	4	20	24	...	74
	Total	103	85	75	87	1	351
	Wages +2	£7.967	£6.694	£5.825	£6.739	...	£27.225
Engines	Floating	...	...	...	...	4	4
	Large Steam	1	1	1	1	...	4
	Small Steam	7	8	6	6	...	27
	Large Manual	13	2	10	12	...	37
	Small Manual	13	18	11	15	...	57
	Total	34	29	28	34	4	129
	Coal	...	...	...	...	£1,000	£1,000
	Repairs + 3	£329	£254	£273	£305	...	£1,161
	Drivers	5	7	5	5	...	22
	Horses	14	16	12	12	...	54
	Drawings + 4	£950	£1,150	£850	£850	...	£3,800
	Total expense	£10.524	£9.370	£7.758	£8.920	...	£36.572

+ 1   Under the head of Rent are included rent, taxes, painting and repairs.

+ 2   Under the head of Wages are included wages as at present, clothing @ £7.10s per man, and surgeon @ £1 per man.

+ 3   Under the head of Repairs to Engines and Renewal of stock combined, are included repairs to hose and small gear generally.

+ 4   Under the head of Drawings are included horses, drivers, and damage from accidents.

1.	Rent	£4,386		10.	Refreshments	£1,000
2.	Salaries	£1,800		11.	Drawings	£3,800
3.	Wages	£27,225		12.	Telegraph	£500
4.	Repairs	£1,161		13.	Sundries	£3,128
5.	Renewal of stock	£1,000		14.	Superannuation	£1,500
6.	Coals	£1,500		15.	Interest on £30.000	£1,500
7.	Calls	£200			@ £5 %	
8.	Turncocks	£300				
9.	Assistants	£1,000				
						£50,000

REDUCED ESTIMATE OF COST OF ESTABLISHING BRIGADE.

Fitting up 4 large Stations	*@ £100*	*£400*	
Fitting up 31 Small Stations	*@ £30*	*£930*	
			£1,330
Fire engines, 3 Floating	*@ £3,000*	*£9,000*	
.. .. *2 Large Land Steamers*	*@ £800*	*£1,600*	
.. .. *30 Small Land Steamers*	*@ £380*	*£11,400*	
.. .. *4 Large Manual Engines*	*@£100*	*£400*	
.. .. *57 Small Manual Engines*	*@ £30*	*£1,710*	
			£24,110
Hose for 3 Floating Steam Engines	*@ £1,000*	*£3,000*	
.. .. *4 Reels*	*@ £250*	*£1,000*	
.. .. *64 Land Steamers*	*@ £100*	*£6,400*	
.. .. *57 Small Manual Engines*	*@ £30*	*£1,710*	
			£12,110
Telegraph, say		*£3,500*	
Sundries		*£950*	
			£4,450
		Total	*£42,000*

Deduct:-   *Probable saving on purchasing partly – used engines and other gear from the present London Fire Engine Establishment and several of the parishes, about-*

£12,000

Leaving the balance of (as the first cost of establishing the new Brigade) about -

£30,000

(you will note that those shown in bold italic are the amendments of the first and second estimate that Captain Shaw had submitted).

Mr. Browne to Mr. Baring MP.
London Fire Engine Establishment, 68 Watling Street.
February 15th 1865.

Sir,
        With reference to former correspondence, I have to inform you that the alterations which Captain Shaw proposes to make in his scheme, &c., in the existing stations, meet with the approval of the Committee of this establishment.

I am, &c.
(signed) W.M Browne, Hon. Sec.

Sir,
        I am directed by Secretary Sir George Grey to acquaint you, for the information of the Lords Commissioners of Her Majesty's Treasury, that he expects to be able shortly to bring in a Bill for the purpose of establishing a fire brigade for the metropolis, under the superintendence of the Metropolitan board of Works, instead of the protection from fire which is now given by a fire brigade maintained voluntarily by the principle Fire Insurance Companies – very efficient indeed in itself, but by no means affording the full amount of protection which is required. In December 1863, Mr Waddington, by direction of Sir George Grey, called the attention of the Lords Commissioners of the Treasury to this subject, and suggested that some contribution in aid of the fire brigade should be made out of the general revenues of the country, in consideration of the protection which would thereby be afforded to a great amount of public property.
        Mr Hamilton stated in reply, that the Lords Commissioners of the Treasury thought that a proposal was "not unreasonable," and that it would best be met by "fixing upon one sum in respect of all public buildings which Parliament might be asked to vote annually, and which should be of such amount as might be considered equitable with reference generally to the extent of the Government property, and to its greater or less risk from fire;" and "that they would be ready to enter further onto the subject on being furnished with fuller particulars as to the measures, and the shape it is to assume."
        Sir George Grey agrees with the opinion expressed by the Lords Commissioners of the Treasury as to the form of the contribution; and the time having now arrived for the settlement of its amount, I am to inform you that, after full consideration, he is of opinion that it might properly be fixed at £10,000 per annum.
        In order to explain the reasons which have induced Sir G.Grey to name that sum, I am to state that the estimate originally framed by Captain Shaw, the Superintendent of the present fire brigade, for the annual cost of an establishment extending over the whole area under the management of the Metropolitan Board of Works, which, as their Lordships are aware, is much more extensive than that comprised under the present arrangements, was £70,000. Sir George Grey has communicated with the Companies who maintain the brigade and with Captain Shaw, in order to ascertain if this estimate could properly be reduced, and he believes that an efficient brigade can be maintained at an annual cost of £50,000, but that no further reduction would be desirable.
        A scheme for a new brigade upon that basis has been prepared and approved by the Companies. This sum will have to be provided by a rate of ½d. in the pound upon the assessment for the poor rate of the Metropolitan district, which will produce about £30,000 per annum, and by a charge of £35 per million of insurances, amounting at present to about £10,000 per annum, which Insurance Companies have agreed to

contribute, as well as to hand over their buildings and staff, free of charge, to the new brigade. These sources of revenue will produce £40,000 per annum, leaving a balance of £10,000 per annum, which if voted by Parliament, would complete the total of £50,000, which is required.

Nothing has been estimated for fines upon the owners of property, both because ratepayers might not unreasonably object to be taxed for the protection of their property from fire, as well as to be liable to fines when the protection for which they have been taxed has actually been afforded to them, and also because it is believed by those whose opinions are entitled to weight, that a system of fines would be injurious to the public interest, as tending to induce persons to conceal as long as possible the outbreak of fire. A small sum may be derived from fines upon fires in chimneys, and this would not materially affect the estimate.

The income, as above estimated, will be a gradually increasing one on account of the extension of building in the neighbourhood of the metropolis, and the probable increase in the amount of property insured; but any additional income which may accrue will not be more than can advantageously be appropriated to the combination of a system of fire escapes with the fire brigade – a most desirable object, and one which Sir George Grey regrets cannot, in his opinion be attained within the limits to which he felt compelled to confine the fist cost of the brigade.

With respect to the additional protection which will be given to public property by the new establishment, I am to point out that no large amount of public property will be situated far from a powerful station.

Taking in the first place public property situated on the banks of the Thames, there are the Victualling – Yard at Deptford, the Tower with its military stores, the Customs – House, Somerset House, the India store Department, the buildings in Whitehall, the Houses of Parliament, Millbank Penitentiary, the Public clothing stores, Chelsea Hospital and the adjacent barracks, all of which are within the reach of powerful floating steam engines.

The present strength of fire engines upon the river is altogether inadequate, consisting of one efficient one inefficient engine. It is proposed to establish four efficient floating steam fire engines on the river, and thus organize a force capable of grappling with those conflagrations which are so disastrous when they occur, and to which so much public property is exposed.

Upon the land new stations will be established at Woolwich, Greenwich, near the British Museum, at Temple Bar, near St James's Palace. Marlborough House and the War Office, Pall Mall, close to the Houses of Parliament, at Pimlico in the neighbourhood of Buckingham Palace, near Kensington Museum, and at Chelsea, thereby affording great additional security to the public property in their vicinity.

Besides the advantage of the existence of the new stations themselves, they will afford facilities for the economical and efficient organization of any special and additional precautions which may be considered desirable for the protection of the public property near them.

These observations will probably be sufficient to prove that the sum recommended is not disproportioned to the additional advantage which will be derived from the new brigade; and if their Lordships desire it , a copy of the scheme which will form the basis of the establishment will be forwarded for their inspection.

It must not be forgotten, however, that no sum is contributed by the public in aid of the present brigade, which protects many public buildings of great importance.

I am to observe in conclusion, that the contribution in aid of the Metropolitan Fire Brigade is somewhat analogous to that which is now made in aid of the Metropolitan Police Rate, and that the sum proposed to be voted in aid of the fire brigade, although actually in the same proportion to the sum raised by rate, ie; in the proportion of one to three, yet when compared with the whole cost of the service, it is less than the sum contributed in aid of the Metropolitan Police, being in the proportion of one to five for the fire brigade, while it is in the proportion of one to four for the police; and moreover, it is to be observed that the contribution in aid of the latter increases with any increase in the proceeds of the rate, while it is proposed that the contribution in aid of the fire brigade be fixed sum.

For the reasons, which I have been directed to explain in this communication, I am to invite the concurrence of the Lords Commissioners of the Treasury in the insertion of a sum of £10,000 in the estimate of the coming year as a contribution in aid of the Metropolitan Fire Brigade.

(signed) T.G.BARING.

Finally after a very long time with several schemes being submitted by Captain Shaw, the Government passed the Metropolitan Fire Brigade Act in 1865. At long last the people of London would get a fire brigade that would cover the whole of London and its suburbs, the firemen would get better fire stations and more up to date equipment.

MAP OF THE LONDON FIRE ENGINE ESTABLISHMENT C1865.

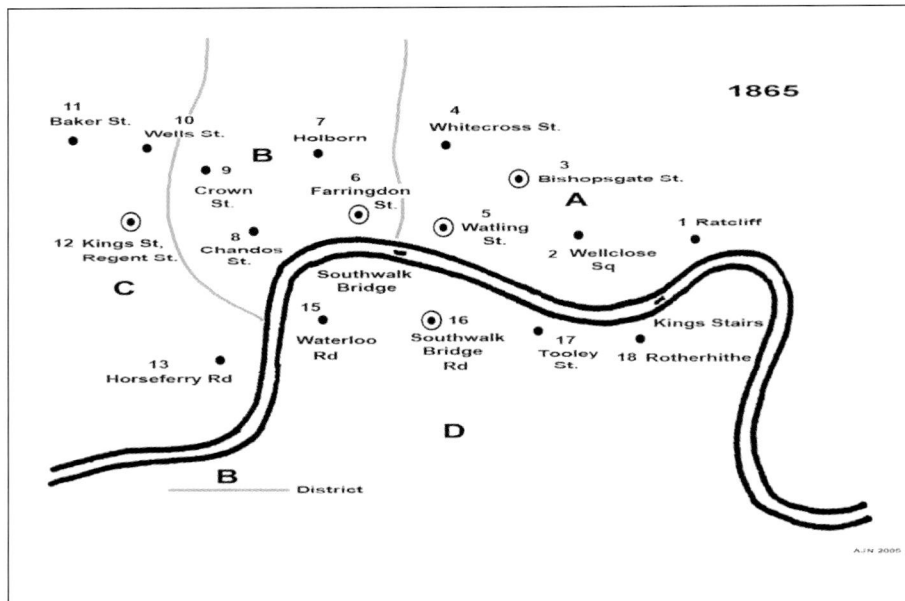

Chandos Street

Photo
Author's Collection

Station No. 8
district B

altered/adapted c1865

1 – steam fire engine
1 – manual escape
1 – hose cart
1 – Station Officer
6 – Firemen
1 – Coachman
1 – pair of horses

*note - the station was
the building to the left
of the arch.
Photo c2003*

Watling Street

Adapted building
c1850s
HQ. LFEE

Station No. 5
district A

Chief Officer
Senior
Superintendents
Station Officer
2 – Coachman
10 – Firemen
1 – large steam fire
engine
2 – small steam fire
engines
1 – manual fire engine

Waterloo Road Fire Station

No. 15 c1865.

station No. F60

2 – steam fire engines
1 – manual escape
1 – hose cart
1 – Station Officer
12 – Firemen
2 – Coachmen
2 – pairs of horses

The Royal Society for the Protection of Life From Fire 1836-1867

IN 1836 a voluntary organisation known as the Society for the Protection of Life from Fire was formed to provide wheeled Fire Escapes at street Fire Stations.

The Royal Society for the Protection of Life from Fire had, in 1857, approved the permanent and efficient maintenance of the following stations in order to have escapes within ¼ of a mile of every dwelling in London; these were placed at Southwark Bridge Road, corner of Union Street, St. George's, corner of Great Dover Street, Newington, opposite the Elephant & Castle, Blackfriars Road, corner of Great Charlotte Street, Lambeth, by the Female Orphan Asylum and at Kennington Cross.

This took the entire number of stations supported by the society to 52, each being attended all night by a well - trained conductor, visited by Inspectors. These arrangements had been carried out by the Committee in the hope of effectually securing the whole of the inhabitants of the Southwark and Lambeth Districts against the dreaded danger of inability to escape from fire.

The Committee felt sure that it required only to be known that these stations, maintained by them at an annual cost of between £80 and £90 each, depended entirely on the support of their respective localities, for the safety and comfort of its inhabitants. The Society felt that no householder could exempt himself from the dangers of fire; 390 fires were attended and 70 lives rescued during the one year alone. This shows how much was the need for public support. During the daytime the Society escapes were parked in church yards and similar open spaces and could not be used, but every evening they were brought out into a prominent position, usually on the junction of two roads and attended throughout the night by an official of the society.

From his report of 1860 Mr. Sampson Low, Jun., Secretary of the Royal Society for the Protection of Life from Fire, stated that there were now 72 stations each attended by a trained conductor, and placed at a distance of not more than half a mile from each other throughout London.

The number of fires attended by the conductors with their fire escapes during the past twelve months had been 524, with 94 lives saved. The society was paid for by public subscription but many still failed to support the society but benefited from the fact that the society was available. It urges people to subscribe. Several parishes paid fixed contributions but passed their responsibility for live saving ladders over to the society.

EXTRACTS FROM ANNUAL REPORT FOR THE YEAR ENDING MARCH 31ST, 1863.

FIRE ESCAPE STATIONS

The Committee have much pleasure in reporting the extension of the Society's arrangements, by six additional Fire Escape stations, making the entire number now supported by the Society, eighty one.

The	76th @ Cobourg Street, Rotherhithe
..	77th @ the Commercial Docks, Rotherhithe
..	78th @ star Corner, Bermondsey
..	79th @ St. James's church, Bermondsey
..	80th in the New Road, Pentonville, corner of Claremont Square
..	81st @ the "Eyre Arms," St.John's Wood.

Each of these stations is attended all night by one of the Society's men, from eight o'clock in the evening in the winter and nine in the summer, to seven o'clock in the morning in winter and six in the summer.

In addition to which they are now arranging for another station in St. John's Wood also one near the Aberdeen Road.

THE FIRE ESCAPE BRIGADE.

The entire force now consists of 94; 84 Conductors on full pay, six supernumeraries, and four Inspectors. It affords the Committee especial satisfaction to report this force in a state of great efficiency, the men are thoroughly practiced in their duties, their vigilance and promptitude have become habitual, whilst continued proofs are being afforded of the intrepid determination with which they devote themselves to the rescue of life in cases of danger.

The continued night tests by sudden calls with systematic competitions for quarterly awards, to the most prompt in each division, works very satisfactory, and with the zealous co-operation of the Inspectors, all seem emulated with one desire to be equal to the shortest time expected for an attendance at a fire.

FIRES ATTENDED DURING THE YEAR
(THE TWELVE MONTHS ENDING MARCH 31ST 1863).

The number of fires attended by the Fire Escape conductors with their Escapes has been 613, exclusive of false alarms and chimneys on fire.

The attendance at these fires has been very prompt and satisfactory, and such as to increase the confidence and feeling of security amongst the inhabitants of the localities of the respective stations. The rare exceptions that ever occur arise from the only cause of complaint with which the committee have had to contend; the want of thought on the part of persons who first discover a fire to run or send to the nearest fire escape station. This should be done before attempting anything else. The stations are so systematically arranged all over London, that, in nine fires out of ten, efficient help and adequate means of safety may now be depended upon within three minutes' run, our men awake, ready, and well provided for any emergency, requiring nothing but to know where they area wanted.

MEASURES TO SECURE THE EARLIEST POSSIBLE CALLS TO FIRE.

In addition to the standing scale of rewards, the Committee take care that any case showing special presence of mind or extra exertion in forwarding a call shall be well rewarded.

Every police Constable has been furnished during the year with a Fire Escape Card, of which 10,000 have been printed and circulated. Special representations have been made to the Police Commissioners, and subsequently a deputation of several of the Committee has had an interview with Sir George Gray, her Majesty's Secretary of state for the Home department, on the subject of securing a more positive order to the Police, that such a "call" on the first alarm should form the primary duty of the first officer at the Fire to see carried out.

These measures, the Committee trust, will all tend to avoid the possibility of future delay in forwarding the first alarm to the Fire Escape Station of the District.

SERVICES RENDERED AND LIVES SAVED.

During the year the Society's men and Fire Escapes have been the direct means of rescuing 67 lives from houses on fire in the metropolis, nearly all of whom, but for the aid thus afforded, must have perished, and in several instances they were only rescued by the imperilment of the lives of those who entered into the burning rooms to search for them. The following is a brief summary of these Fires;-

Date 1862	No. of case	Premises on fire	Conductor & Fire Escape attending	Persons Rescued	Remarks on official report
May 11th	7272	67 London Road	Semmens – Newington	6	Rescued from imminent death by fire, five of the inmates being taken from their beds whilst the premises on fire
July 21st	7411	17 Piccadilly	Arnold – Piccadilly	2	Saved from what appeared inevitable death, and at great risk to Conductor
Aug 22nd	7450	20 Old Street St. Lukes	Shaw – Aldersgate Street	2	Save by escape entirely
Nov 17th	7604	4 Dean Street	Briggs – Finsbury Steer – Bishopgate Street	10	Saved entirely by the intrepid exertions of the Conductors
Dec 26th	7672	6 Portland Street Soho	Clarke – Dean Street Soho	2	Rescued by means of escape, after great exertions and at severe personal injuries to the Conductor

The details of each of the above cases are given in the Society's Annual Report, a copy of which may be obtained upon application at the office, 14 Ludgate Hill.

In 1865 the total cost of the scheme was £8,500 per annum. 85 street escape stations were maintained and manned by attendants at £100 per annum.

Chapter 2

Metropolitan Fire Brigade (MFB) (Metropolitan Board of Works) 1866-1889

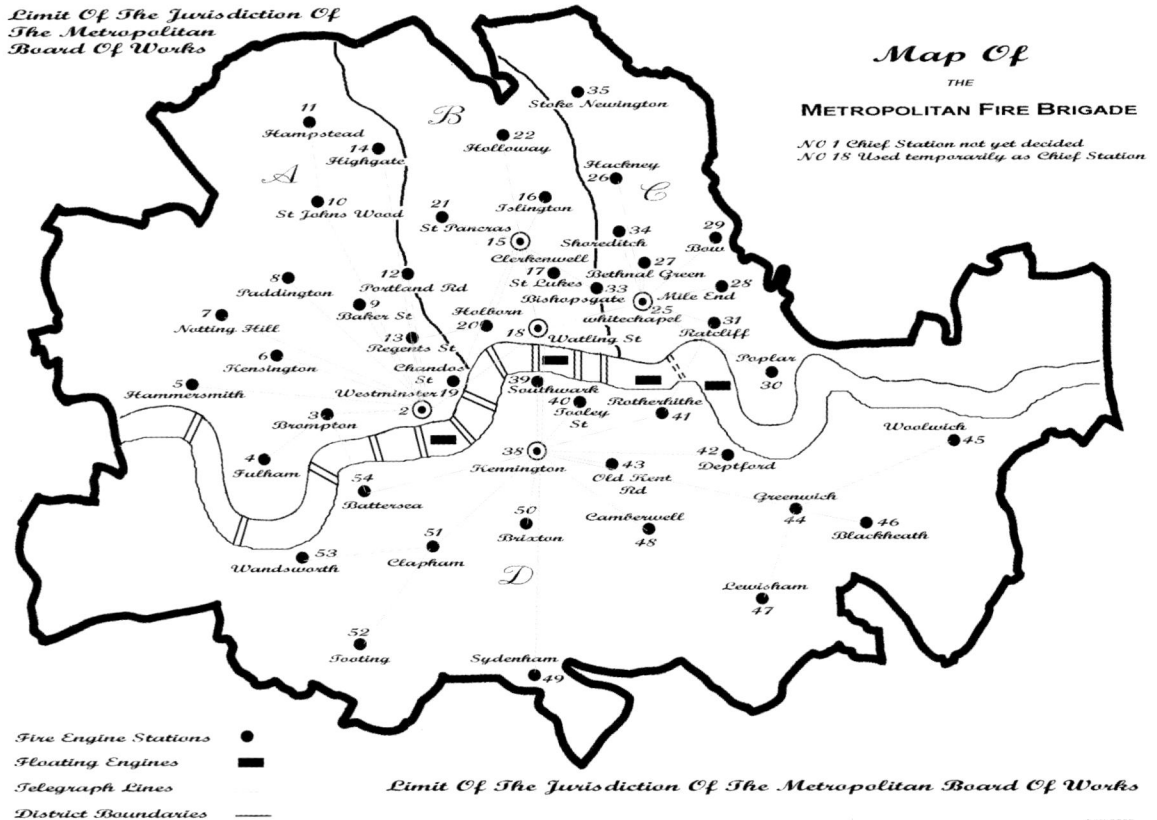

Map of the Metropolitan Fire Brigade.

The new Fire Brigade took over from the LFFE on the 1st of January 1866. In the annual reports of the Metropolitan Board of Works the following pages show the progress made in station building and the gradual build-up of the new brigade. The LFEE handed over to the Board 1 Floating steam engine lying off Southwark Bridge, 4 land steamers and 27 manual engines. The Board purchased 11 new land steamers and 23 manual engines, which they have purchased from the Parishes. They also continued to hire the steam engines held by the LFEE, the large steamer kept on board the barge off Rotherhithe and used for the protection of the waterside properties, and 4 land steamers. The number of men transferred on 1st January 1866 was 130. The Metropolitan Board of Works Report of 1865-66 listed the following fire stations.

118 Cock Hill Ratcliff. E1
23 Bishopsgate Street. Without
27 Farringdon Street. EC4
44 Chandos Street. WC2

Wells Street / Oxford Street.
39 King Street / Golden Square. W1
142 Waterloo Road. SE1
165 Tooley Street. SE1

20 / 21 Wellclose Square. E1
64 Whitecross Street . EC1
254 High Holborn.
George Yard / Crown Street.
Soho
33 King Street / Baker Street.
Horseferry Road Westminster.
102 Southwark Bridge Road. SE1
6 Lucas Street. Rotherhithe.

2 Floating Stations ;   @ Southwark Bridge.
                             @ Rotherhithe.

In order to ensure the immediate and as far as possible, proper protection of London, arrangements were made with the parishes that had a proper engine and staff to maintain them and continue to cover that part of London, until such time that the brigade could take over with new fire stations. The following list is of stations available under the agreement.

Camden Town.	Church Street.	Bethnal Green.
South Kensington.	Limehouse Church.	Hammersmith
Millwall (Mr Roberts).	Paddington Green.	Whitechapel Church
Royal Oak Bayswater.	Shoreditch.	St. Johns Wood Road.
Globe Fields, Mile End.	Sloane Square.	Greenwich.
Fulham Road.	Deptford (Messrs Penn & Son).	Islington, Florence Street.
Peckham.	Holloway Road.	Wandsworth.
Hackney Town Hall.	Brixton.	Stoke Newington.
Lewisham.	De Beauvoir Town.	South Hackney.
Bow.		

The Board also established a small station at Poplar.
The duties of some of the above stations were to be taken over by the MFB.

1866-67. The Brigade was divided into districts, with new stations included in the list

DISTRICT "A"

Marylebone.	33 Kings Street / Baker Street.	
Highgate.	Junction Place Highgate Road.	
Oxford Street.	76 Wells Street.	
Regent Street.	39 King Street, Golden Square.	
Westminster.	Horseferry Road, Regents Street.	
Chelsea.	Draycott Place, Sloane Square.	*
Brompton.	Britten Street, nr Kings Road.	*
Kensington.	Lower Phillimore Mews, Hornton Street.	*
Hammersmith.	Brooke Green Lane, Broadway.	
Notting Hill.	Ladbrooke Grove.	*
Bayswater.	Queens Mews, Queens Road.	*
Paddington.	Hermitage Street. Paddington Green. (photo)	
St.Johns Wood.	Wellington Road.	*

DISTRICT "B"

Farringdon Street.	27½ Farringdon Street.	
Islington.	Florence Street, Upper Street.	*
St.Lukes.	64 Whitecross Street.	
City.	66 - 69 Watling Street. (Chief Station). (photo)	
Charing Cross.	44 Chandos Street. (photo)	
Holborn.	254 High Holborn.	
St.Giles.	George Yard, Crown Street.	
St.Pancras.	King Road. (adjacent to the workhouse).	

DISTRICT "C"

St.George in the east.	20 - 21 Wellclose Square.	
Bethnal Green.	72 Bethnal Green Road.	
Hackney .	Old Town Hall.	*
South Hackney.	Percy Road, Wells Street.	*
Mile End.	Frimley Street, Alderney Road.	*
Bow.	8 Winnington Place, Devon's Road.	*
Ratcliff.	118 Lock Hill.	
Poplar.	Newby Place.	*
Bishopsgate.	23 Bishopsgate Street, Without.	
Shoreditch.	7 Kingsland Road.	*
De Beauvoir Town.	St.Peter Road.	*
Stoke Newington.	High Street.	*
Whitechapel.	Church Lane.	

DISTRICT "D"

Kennington.	Lower Kennington Lane.	
Tooley Street.	165 Tooley Street.	
Rotherhithe.	6 Lucas Street.	*
Greenwich.	35 Blisset Street.	
Peckham.	Blue Anchor Yard, High Street.	*
Waterloo.	142 Waterloo Road. (photo)	
Southwark.	102 Southwark Bridge Road.	

Those marked * are stations which the Board have established for the temporary protection of several neighbourhoods until stations of a permanent nature were established. The following sites were obtained for the erection of fire stations.

Westminster.	Nr Victoria Street.
Marylebone.	Charlotte Street, Portland Road.
St.John's Wood.	Adelaide Road.
Chelsea.	South Parade.
Fulham.	Walham Green.
Hampstead.	High Street.
Islington.	Asteys Row, Essex Road.
Shoreditch.	Old Street Road.
Bow.	Bow Road.
Poplar.	West India Dock Road.
Kennington.	Lower Kennington Lane.
Old Kent Road.	Old Kent Road.
Brixton.	Shepherds Lane.

Camberwell.	Peckham.
Deptford.	Evelyn Street.
Sydenham.	Adjoining Crystal Palace.
Lewisham.	Rushey Green.

The Board also intended to erect stations, on ground that belonged to them, at Southwark Street, Rotherhithe and Woolwich.

From the 1st July 1867 the Metropolitan Board of Works committee agreed to take over the whole of the Royal Society for the Protection of Life from Fire, including equipment and several of their fire escape conductors (67) and 85 of the street stations.

By 1868 Massey Shaw was already telling the committee that the Headquarters at the city station, Watling Street was now too small and that he wanted a larger Headquarters near to the Thames to house all his departments, training section and a fireboat. A site was found along the Victoria Embankment but proved to be too expensive and eventually the site at Southwark Bridge Road was found.

The contracts for the stations at Westminster, Chelsea, Poplar, Brixton, and Camberwell had been let and some progress already made in the building work. By 1868 these stations were completed and occupied.

During the period of 1868 - 69 Islington, and Wandsworth (in the High street) the station in South Parade Chelsea, and at Camden Town, Lewisham and Old Kent Road had all been completed and some occupied.

Stations at St.Johns Wood, Fulham, Shorditch, Bow, Southwark Street, Clapham, and Sydenham were being built and premises at Hampstead (formerly a police station) had also been purchased by the Board.

By now the Brigade had four river stations one for each district, off Millbank, off Southwark Bridge, in Limehouse Reach and off a platform at Rotherhithe.

Stations in the 'A' district; Fulham, Hampstead, in the 'C' district; Hackney, Bow, Shoreditch; in the 'D' district; Southwark Street, Old Kent Road, Tooting, Sydenham, Rushey Green Lewisham, and Woolwich all opened during 1869. Stations at Kennington and St Johns Wood were in the course of erection. All principal fire stations were now equipped with both steam and manual engines.

During 1869-70 stations at St Johns Wood and Kennington opened; The Board commenced the erection of, and some re-construction work to stations at Deptford, Paddington, Notting Hill and Wandsworth. A site was secured at Blackheath and endeavours were made to secure sites for Clerkenwell, Mile End and Battersea.

The Board decided to discontinue the stations from the LFEE at Waterloo Road and Crown Street Soho and the station at Clerkenwell will substitute Farringdon Street.

1870-71; on the opening of the stations at King Street Kensington, Ladbroke Road Notting Hill, Evelyn Street Deptford and Camden Town, the LFEE stations at Kensington, Notting Hill, Bayswater and St Pancras will close. Blackheath now in course of construction and the Holloway site soon to begin, and the sites now acquired for Clerkenwell, Mile End and Battersea.

The Metropolitan Board of Works architect Mr Cresy died in 1870 and Mr Mott was transferred to the department as his successor. The station at Hermitage Street, Paddington Green, was altered and those at King Street, Kensington, and Tranquil Vale, Blackheath, now under construction, these both being opened by 1871. Holloway, Battersea and Clerkenwell by now being erected and the Mile End station to replace the existing building.

1872 saw the opening of Holloway and Mile End which allowed the station at Frimley Street to close and a proposal to build a fire station in Commercial Road to replace Wellclose Square.

1873; Clerkenwell opened on 24th May and the station on the lower Wandsworth Road, Battersea, was nearly completed. Hampstead station was entirely re-built, Whitecross Street in course of reconstruction (the old station being taken down and finished by November 1874.)

1874, Battersea was opened in March and the stations at South Hackney and De Beauvoir Town closed, both of which were old parish engine houses from 1866. The building at Waterloo Road was converted into workshops. Land leased at corner of East Ferry Road / West Ferry Road for Isle of Dogs station. The Board made reference to a station at entrance to West India Docks; photos show this building to have been occupied both by the Metropolitan Fire Brigade known as poplar FS, and the London Salvage Corps. Whitecross Street opened, Whitechapel was being erected and Tooley Street and Portland Road were altered and repaired; Sydenham, Kennnington and Chandos Street being repaired.

1875, Workshops opened, Rotherhithe work commenced and both Poplar and Bishopsgate were repaired throughout.

1876, new station to be built at Brook Green Lane Hammersmith in place of the present temporary station which is close by. In June the MBW agreed to purchase property at Winchester House in Southwark Bridge Road comprising 1¾ acres for £35,000. Isle of dogs nearly completed and Highgate, Islington and Wandsworth all altered and repaired.

Gradually over the years the brigade increased in size and efficiency, more Steam Fire Engines were purchased and still more fire stations built. By 1877 Shaw had 48 Fire Engine Stations, 107 Fire Escape Stations and 4 Floating Stations, 3 Floating Steam Fire Engines, 1 Iron Barge to carry a land Steam Fire Engine, 5 Large Land Steam Fire Engines and 21 Small Land Steam Fire Engines. They also had 14 7in Manual Fire Engines, 58 6in Manual Fire Engines and 20 under 6in Manual Fire Engines and 130 Fire Escapes with a establishment of over 400 Firemen including the Chief Officer and Superintendents. During this time the firemen lived at the stations as did those that were married, with their families, though due to lack of space at some stations men were boarded out to nearby premises.

1877, Rotherhithe opened in May replacing the small engine house in Lucas Road (formerly LFEE of 1866). Hammersmith in Brook Green Road built for £4,120 by Messrs, Hook & Oldrey, occupied in June and the small building in The Broadway vacated. Isle of Dogs built for £3,133 by Mr W.D Tink occupied also in June and the Bow Road Station which had been built in 1869 now enlarged at a cost of £2,983.The contract for adapting the existing buildings and erection of the new HQ for the Brigade was given to Messrs, Hook & Oldrey the agreed price being £27,798 - a total cost of £70,000.

1878, by 1st June, Southwark was occupied and the station in Southwark Street closed but the men from the 'B' floating engine which lies in the river near Southwark Bridge were still housed there. The City Corporation had been unhappy that Shaw moved his HQ out of the city stating that most fires were in the city and that he was building stations out in the suburbs. They at considerable cost had installed fire hydrants which were available at all times to fight fires and demanded that the Brigade should revise its organisation to take advantage of the improved facilities. Shaw had to introduce makeshift measures to satisfy the Corporation.

Being unable to build permanent fire stations he introduced the temporary movable stations. These small stations on wheels could be pulled by horse and set up in appointed positions at night. They were designed to accommodate two men and their equipment, the first was placed at Ludgate Circus in 1879 with others placed at strategic sites, but by 1882 under pressure from the City Corporation were manned day and night.

Each of these street stations had a hose cart that carried 300ft of hose and the tools required for the fireman to get to work. On receipt of a fire call the first fireman would rush off with the hose cart while the other fireman would wait until enough help arrived to push the escape. Usually a fireman with his hose cart arrived first and was able to get a jet to work before the local fire station arrived.

Some of these hose carts were stationed at some of the City police stations and by doing so pleased the City Corporation. The following list shows the increase over the years of the street stations and hose carts.

1880 moveable station	1 hose cart	17
1881	5	17
1882	11	29
1883	12	52
1884	12	61
1885	23	62
1886	26	64
1887	26	63
1888	27	74
1889	27	80

Street escape stations were also increased and the manpower increased from 395 men in 1879 to 591 men in 1889. During the same period the fire stations also increased from 53 to 55. The main fire stations were responsible for up to six street stations.

Shooters Hill is in course of erection by Messrs, Hook & Oldrey at a cost of £4,945 and Greenwich which will replace the parochial engine house the land in Grove Street being purchased for £750 in 1876 to replace Blisset Street.

The brigade supplied a moveable fire station to replace the station closed at Farringdon Street.

A fire station will be built in the neighborhood of Knightsbridge, the lease of premises suitable for the purpose purchased for £2, 900; they consist of a house in Chapel Place and the street situated between Brompton Road & Knightsbridge Road, and stables and coachhouse in Relton Mews. The building work will be done by Mr.C.W.Reading for £1,192.

1879, stations occupied at Chapel Place at the back of Brompton Road, Knightsbridge, and those at Shooters Hill and Grove Road Greenwich. Fire station being erected at Tooley Street and a station proposed at Pavilion Road off Sloane Square, Chelsea.

A few days following the opening of the Shooters Hill fire station, a serious accident occurred when the engine and horses were out on exercise. Whilst descending Constitution Hill and about quarter of a mile from the station, the brake refused to work. The driver did his best to pull up the two horses, but the hill being so steep, the horses were unable to check the speed. In turning a sharp corner opposite the Eagle tavern the firemen aboard were thrown from the engine into the road. The captain of the station had his leg broken, and the firemen received severe cuts and bruises. The horses continued at a furious pace down the hill to the Royal Military Academy, where the engine overturned in front of the Governor's residence. The engine, which was new, was badly damaged, and one of the horses received serious injuries and had to be put down.

1880, Tooley Street opened, the former LFEE station at Holborn to be replaced by one at Theobalds Road. Land for a station at Norwood purchased for £580, and the stations at Camberwell and Holloway to be enlarged, an additional floor to be added to the Holloway station. Notice served on the Board by London & Chatham Railway to demolish Grove Street fire station to enable them to extend the line at Blackheath Hill to Stockwell Street, Greenwich.

The moveable fire station supplied in 1879 has proved to be a success, now these type of stations will be situated at Ludgate Circus, St.Clement Danes Church in the Strand, Holborn Circus, Tower Hill near the Royal Mint and at Vauxhall Cross, with six more on order. These will be so placed as to sub-divide the distances between the fire engine stations in the parts of London where a prompt attendance is required.

1881, the station at Pavilion Road opened in June, with a station at Shadwell in Glamis Road to be built to replace the station at Broad Street, Ratcliffe and to house the men from the 'C' floating engine.

Norwood now being built and the station at Chandos Street c1835 to close and a new station to be built at Gt. Scotland Yard, also the station at Highgate Road Kentish Town, a parochial engine of St.Pancras, is due to close. Two fire stations in Kensington possibly at King Street and at Ladbroke Road. Land purchased at Faraday Road for £1.250. Proposals to extend the fire station and headquarters at Southwark. Other stations proposed in 1881 were at Bishopsgate, Regent Street, Baker Street, Camden Town, Stoke Newington and at Bethnal Green.

1882, the station at Norwood was now in use. Southwark HQ enlarged at a cost of £23,000.

1884, Scotland Yard station opened.

1886, November 10th Fire Station opened at Leswin Road Stoke Newington, the station in the High Street closed and Holborn station opened.

1887, Gt. Marlborough Street opened, new station proposed at Blanford Street and will be called Manchester Square fire station. The station at Sunbury Street Woolwich opened.

In 1888 the Local Government Act was passed and in 1889 the new London County Council took over the Brigade.

Westminster

Photo No. LFB
collection (NF)
B 1867

Station No.2
district A
c1876

c 1892

1 – steam fire engine
1 – horsed escape
1 – manual fire engine
1 – hose cart
1 – Station Officer
12- Firemen
2 – Coachmen
2 – pair of horses

Camberwell

B 1867

Station No. 2
district A
c1876
Superintendents
Station.

c 1892
1 – steam fire engine
1 – horsed escape
1 – manual fire engine
1 – hose cart
1 – Station Officer
12 – Firemen
2 – Coachmen
2 – pairs of horses

Brixton

B1867
Station No. 50
district D
c1876

c 1892
1 – steam fire engine
1 – horsed escape
1 – manual escape
1 – hose cart
1 – Station Officer
11- Firemen
2 – Coachmen
2 – pairs of horses

Bow Photo

B 1867
Station No. 29
district C
c1876.

c 1908
1 – steam fire engine
1 – Station Officer
1 – horsed escape
11 – Firemen
1 – manual escape
2 – Coachmen
1 – hose cart
2 – pairs of horses

Hackney

B1867
Station No.26
district C
c1876

c 1908
1 – steam fire engine
1 – horsed escape
1 – manual escape
1 – hose cart
1 – Station Officer
10 - Firemen
2 – Coachmen
2 – pair of horses

Rushey Green

B1867
Station No. 47
district D
c1876

c 1908
1 – horsed escape
1 – manual escape
1 – hose cart
1 – hose tender
1 – Station Officer
5 – Firemen
1 – Coachman
2 – pair of horses

Old Kent Road

B1868
Station No.43
district D
c1876

c1892
1 – steam fire engine
1 – manual engine
1 – manual escape
1 – hose cart
1 – Station Officer
8 – Firemen
1 – Coachman
1 – pair of horses

Southwark Street

Photo
Author's Collection
B 1868

1 – steam fire engine
1 – horsed escape
1 – manual escape
1 – hose cart
1 – Station Officer
11 – Firemen
2 – Coachmen
2 – pair of horses

Kennington

Photo Lambeth
Borough Council
Achives
B1868

Station No. 38
district D
c1876

Superintendents
Station

c1892
1 – steam fire engine
1 – horsed escape
1 – manual
1 – hose cart
1 – Station Officer
11 – Firemen
2 – Coachmen
2 – pair of horses

Clapham

B 1868
Station No.51
district D
c1876

c1892
1 – steam fire engine
1 – horsed escape
1 – manual
1 – hose cart
1 – Station Officer
11 – Firemen
2 – Coachmen
2 – pairs of horses

Portland Road

B 1868
Station 12
district A
c1876

c 1892
1 – manual fire engine
1 – manual escape
1 – hose cart
1 – Station Officer
5 - Firemen

Notting Hill

B 1868
Station 7
district A
c1876

c1908
1 – steam fire engine
1 – horsed escape
1 – manual escape
1 – hose cart
1 – Station Officer
9 – Firemen
2 – Coachmen
2 – pairs of horses

Poplar

B 1868
Station No. 30
district C
c1876

c1908
1 – steam fire engine
1 – horsed escape
1 – manual escape
1 – hose cart
1 – Station Officer
12 – Firemen
2 – Coachmen
2 – pairs of horses

Sydenham

B 1868
Station No.49
district D
c1876

c1908
1 – manual fire engine
1 – horsed escape
1 – curricle engine
1 – manual escape
1 – Station Officer
6 – Firemen
1 – Coachman
1 – pair of horses

Tooting

B1869
Station No. 52
district D
c1876

c1908
1 – steam fire engine
1 – horsed escape
1 – manual escape
1 – hose cart
1 – Station Officer
12 – Firemen
2 – Coachmen
2 – pairs of horses

Paddington
(Hermitage St)

B 1870
Station No. 8
district A
c1876

1 – steam fire engine
1 – manual escape
1 – hose cart
1 – Station Officer
6 – Firemen
1 – Coachman
1 – pair of horses

Hampstead

B1871
Station No. 11
district A
c1876

c1908
1 – steam fire engine
1 – horsed escape
1 – hose cart
1 – station Officer
9 – Firemen
2 – Coachmen
2 – pairs of horses

*The horsed escape is
kept in the station and
the steam engine in the
Holly Bush Hill
premises.*

Holly Bush Hill.
(Hampstead)

St.John's Wood

B1871
Station No.10
district A
c1876

c1908
1 – steam fire engine
1 – horsed escape
1 – manual escape
1 – hose cart
1 – Station Officer
8 – Firemen
1 – Coachman
1 – pair of horses

Kensington

B1872
Station No. 6
district A
c1876

c1900
1 – steam fire engine
1 – manual engine
1 – manual escape
1 – hose cart
1 – Station Officer
8 – Firemen
1 – Coachman
1 – pair of horses

Deptford

B1872

Station No. 42
district D
c1876

c1900
1 – steam fire engine
1 – manual engine
1 – manual escape
1 – hose cart
1 – Station Officer
8 – Firemen
1 – Coachman
1 – pair of horses

Blackheath

B1872
station No. 46
district D
c1876

c1908
1 – horsed escape
1 – manual escape
1 – hose cart
1 – Station Officer
7 – Firemen
1 – Coachman
1 – pair of horses

Holloway

B1872
Station 22
district B
c1876

c1908
1 – steam fire engine
1 – horsed escape
1 – manual escape
1 – manual fire engine
1 – hose cart
1 – Station Officer
10 – Firemen
2 – Coachmen
2 – pairs of horses

Mile End

B1872
Station No. 28
district C
c1876

c1908
1 – steam fire engine
1 – Horsed escape
1 – manual escape
1 – hose cart
1 – Station Officer
11 – Firemen
2 – Coachmen
2 – pairs of horses

Battersea

B1872
Station 54 D
c1876
Station enlarged &
altered 1898 – 9

c1908
1 – steam fire engine
1 – horsed escape
1 – hose cart
1 – Station Officer
9 – Firemen
2 – Coachmen
2 – pairs of horses

Whitechapel

Superintendents
station
Enlarged 1900.

Whitechapel

B1874
Station No. 25
district C
c1876

c1908
1 – steam fire engine
1 – horsed escape
1 – horsed long ladder
1 – manual escape
1 – hose cart
1 – hose & coal van
1 – trap
1 – Superintendent
1 – station Officer
16 – Firemen
3 – Coachmen
3 – pairs of horses

Rotherhithe

B1875
Station No. 41
district D
c1876

c1908
1 –steam fire engine
1 – horsed escape
1 – manual escape
1 – hose cart
1 – Station Officer
11 – Firemen
2 – Coachmen
2 – pairs of horses

Hammersmith

Station No. 5
district A.
c1876

c 1908
1 – steam fire engine
1 – horsed escape
1 – long ladder
1 – hose cart
1 – Station Officer
10 – Firemen
2 – Coachmen
2 – pairs of horses

Southwark Chief Station

B1876
station No.F1
c1876
Alan Gilfrin collection.

c1908
2 – motor fire engines
1 – horsed escape
1 – hose van
in addition there are in reserve
and for training
1 – horsed escape
3 – manual engines
13 – manual escapes
1 – hose and ladder truck
1 – motor tractor
1 – oil wagon
1 – canteen van

1 – steam fire engine
1 – turntable long ladder
1 – motor car
8 – steam fire-engines

2 – long ladders
11 – hose carts
3 – hose and coal vans
1 – locomobile
2 – store vans
2 – trollies

Chief Officer
1 – Divisional Officer (south)
1 – Senior Superintendent
9 – Station Officers
42 – Firemen
14 – Coachmen
5 – pairs of horses

Southwark Headquarters

HQ building at far end and built
in front of Winchester House
which still exists today. The HQ
building was damaged during the
war and was eventually
demolished.
In the foreground Engine House
and gates into the drill yard. The
present station was built
adjoining the entrance block, the
gates are now below an arch
forming part of the new station.

Isle of Dogs.

B1877
Station No. 35
district C
c1894

c1900
1 – steam fire engine
1 – horsed escape
1 – hose cart
1 – Station Officer
9 – Firemen
2 – Coachmen
2 – pairs of horses

Knightsbridge

B1879
Station No. 5
district A
c1894

c1900
1 – steam fire engine
1 – manual engine
1 – manual escape
1 – hose cart
1 – Station Officer
10 – Firemen
1 – Coachman
1 – pair of horses

Shooters Hill

B1879
Station No. 44
district D
c1894

c1908
1 – steam fire engine
1 – manual escape
1 – hose & ladder van
1 – hose cart
1 – Station Officer
9 – Firemen
2 – Coachmen
2 – pairs of horses

Greenwich

B1879
Station No. 43
district D
c1894

c1908
1 – steam fire engine
1 – horsed escape
1 – manual escape
1 – hose cart
1 – Station Officer
11 – Firemen
2 – Coachmen
2 – pairs of horses

Tooley Street

B1879
Station No. 51
district E
c1894

c1908
1 – steam fire engine
1 – horsed escape
1 – long ladder
1 – hose cart
1 – Station Officer
11 – Firemen
2 – Coachmen
2 – pairs of horses

Chelsea

B1880
Station No. 4
district A
c1894

c1908
1 – steam fire engine
1 – horsed escape
1 – hose cart
1 – Station Officer
9 – Firemen
2 – Coachmen
2 – pairs of horses

West Norwood

B1881
Station No. 54
district E
c1894

c1908
1 – steam fire engine
1 – horsed escape
1 – manual escape
1 – hose cart
1 – Station Officer
9 – Firemen
2 – Coachmen
2 – pairs of horses

Holborn

B1881
Station No. 21
district B
c1894

c1908
1 – steam fire engine
1 – horsed escape
1 – long ladder
1 – manual escape
1 – hose cart
1 – Station Officer
17 – Firemen
3 – Coachmen
3 – pairs of horses

Scotland Yard

B1881
Station No. 20
district B
c1894

c1908
1 – steam fire engine
1 – horsed escape
1 – long ladder
1 – hose cart
1 – Station Officer
11 – Firemen
2 – Coachmen
2 – pairs of horses

Shadwell

B1881
Station No. 34
district C
c1894

c1908
1 – steam fire engine
1 – horsed escape
1 – horsed long ladder
1 – manual escape
1 – hose cart
1 – Station Officer
13 – Firemen
3 – coachmen
3 – pairs of horses

North Kensington

B 1882
Station No. 12
district A
c1894

c1908
1 – steam fire engine
1 – horsed escape
1 – manual escape
1 – hose cart
1 – hose tender
1 – Station Officer
11 – Firemen
2 – Coachmen
2- pairs of horses

c1965
GLC part of Northern
Command A division
station No. A29
1 – pump escape
1 - pump
1 – Station Officer
1 – Sub Officer
1 – Leading Fireman
11 - Firemen

Kentish Town

B 1883
Station No. 25
district B
c 1894
c 1908
1 – steam fire engine
1 – horsed escape
1 – manual escape
1 – hose cart
1 – hose tender (spare)
1 – Station Officer
15 – Firemen
2 – Coachmen
2 – pairs of horses

c1965
GLC part of Eastern
Command
C division
station C29
1 – pump escape
1 – pump
1 – Station Officer
1 – Sub Officer
1 – Leading Fireman
11 – Firemen

Bishopsgate

B 1884   1 – steam fire engine
Station No. 36   1 – horsed escape
district C   1 – hose tender
c1894   1 – long ladder
c1908   1 – manual escape
                          1 – hose cart
                          1 –Station Officer
                          20 – Firemen
                          4 – Coachmen
                          3 – pairs of horses

Camden town

B1885
Station No. 24
district B
c1894

c 1908
1 – steam fire engine
1 – horsed escape
1 – horsed long ladder
2 – manual escapes
1 – hose cart
1 – canteen van
1 – Station Officer
15 – Firemen
5 – Coachmen
3 – pairs of horses

c1965
GLC part of Northern
Command A division
station No. A22
1 – pump escape
1 – pump
1 – Station Officer
1 – Sub Officer
1 – Leading Fireman
11 – Firemen

Stoke Newington

B1885
enlarged 1902
Station No. 38
district C
c1894

c1908
1 – steam fire engine
1 – horsed escape
1 – manual escape
1 – hose cart
1 – Station Officer
11 – Firemen
2 – Coachmen
2 – pairs of horses

c1965
GLC part of Eastern
Command
C division
station No. C23
1 – pump escape
1 – pump
1 – Station Officer
1 – Sub Officer
1 – Leading Fireman
11 - Firemen

Woolwich

B1887
Station No. 42
district D
c1894

c1908
1 – steam fire engine
1 – horsed escape
1 – manual escape
1 – hose cart
1 – Station Officer
9 – Firemen
2 – Coachmen
2 – pairs of horses

enlarged 1910

c1965
GLC
part of Southern
Command
E division
station No. E24

1 – pump escape
1 – pump
1 – fireboat crew
1 – Station Officer
1 – Sub Officer
1 – Leading Fireman
19 – Firemen

c2004
LFEPA
Part of Southern
Command
station No. E24

1 – pump ladder
1 – Sub Officer
1 – Leading Firefighter
7 - Firefighters

Gt. Marlborough Street

B1887
Station No. 22
district B
c1894

c1908
1 – steam fire engine
1 – horsed escape
1 – manual escape
1 – hose cart
1 – Station Officer
15 – Firemen
2 – Coachmen
2 – pairs of horses

Chapter 3

London Fire Brigade
London County Council (LCC) 1889-1965

21st March 1889, The control of the Metropolitan Fire Brigade changed from The Metropolitan Board of Works to the London County Council.

1889 July 29th the opening of a Fire Station at Globe Road junction of Roman Road Bethnal Green.

1890; Manchester Square Fire Station built at a cost of £13. 878 of 12000sq feet, in Chiltern Street leading from Marylebone Road and Blandford Street parallel to Baker Street. Chief Headquarters of 'A' division comprising Marylebone, Hampstead, Westminster and Fulham. The Headquarters for 20 years transferred from Westminster Fire Station to Manchester Square.

The Fire Brigade Committee were informed that five new moveable stations at a cost of £170 with fire extinguishing appliances were ready and it was proposed to place them at Hyde park Corner, Tottenham Court Road near Whitefields chapel, City Road, Aldgate High Street and Newington near the Elephant & Castle. It was also recommended that to enable the moveable stations to be worked properly that 25 men be added to the staff of the Brigade, enabling 5 men per station. The committee accepted the report.

1891; The foundation stone for the Wandsworth Fire Station located at Lebanon Gardens near the existing station was laid, designed by the council architect Mr Blashill. The site cost £1,000 and £7,980 to build and was completed in 1892.

October 31st, Captain Shaw relinquished his duties as Chief Officer of the MFB. Mr. J,Sexton Simmonds was appointed Chief Officer of the Brigade.

July 1892 the tender received from Messrs Stimpson & Co to build the Dulwich Fire Station for £10,260 was accepted. In the October 50 firemen had volunteered to form the Brigades Brass Band.

1893 a site at Victoria Embankment near to Blackfriars Bridge was purchased, this would allow the station at Watling Street to close. Land at Tabernacle Walk obtained to replace the station at Shoreditch. In August the Fire Brigade Committee stated that it intended to compulsory purchase Nos, 492-494-496-498 Edgware Road to build Paddington Fire Station. The duty at the Dulwich station commenced on 31st July.

1894, at a recent meeting of the Streatham Ratepayers Association, it was decided to ask the County Council to provide a Fire Station and the necessary call points for Streatham.

Proposals are before the LCC to provide six fire stations and 128 sub-stations at a cost of £92,570 and involving an annual expenditure of £24,300.

Additional duties during the year were commenced, 5 duties with hose carts and escapes or hose and ladder trucks, 3 duties with hose carts at existing escape duties, and 15 duties with escapes only. The duties at St. Clement Danes Strand, St. James' Church Bermondsey, Vauxhall Cross and Streatham, which were formerly done by night only, are now available night and day. A temporary duty by night and during the day with a hose and ladder truck is now being done at North Woolwich, pending the erection of a sub - station. The duty with a hose cart by night at St.Dunstan's Church, Fleet Street, has been discontinued.

A steam fire engine has been added to each of the following stations, St. John's Wood, Bethnal Green, Isle of Dogs and West Norwood, and one has been ordered for the Notting Hill station, though alterations will have to made before it is placed there.

The Chief Officer in his report for the year 1894 stated that he hoped the entire sub - stations and street stations authorised by the council will be built during the coming months. The number of firemen employed was 111 by day and 359 by night, a total of 470 in every 24 hours, and an average of 360 available at night to fight fires.

The station at New Cross opened on 16th June as the superintendent's station for the D district, the street station duty at Commercial Road, the hose cart and escape duty at Nunhead and the escape duty at Queen's Road, with 12 firemen, 1 coachman, 2 horses and one steam fire engine were added to the Brigade strength.

The LCC have decided to place a hose and ladder fire truck with watch box for the MFB in the Beckenham Road, Penge. Extension to Kennington Fire Station being done by Works Dept at a cost of £1,400.

At the meeting of the LCC on July 24th the Chairman Sir John Hutton delivered his annual address.

He stated that during the year fire stations had been opened at Trafalgar Square Brompton, Dulwich, New Cross and Rotherhithe. New stations will be built at Islington, Lewisham and Paddington and the station at Hampstead, Clerkenwell, Kennnington and Battersea to be enlarged to provide quarters for between 300-400 married men. New sub - stations to be built at North Woolwich and at Battersea.

It was reported that one evening shortly before midnight, whilst getting himself a drink from the kitchen on the ground floor at the Bow Fire Station, a fireman heard a fall outside in the drill yard.

He found one of his mates lying in a heap, (the injured fireman) was removed to the London Hospital where he was found to have a fatal fracture to the skull.

At the inquest the Coroner was told that all firemen had to be back at their stations by 10: 30 pm, but the fireman had climbed over the wall in a drunken state and fallen.

1896, The LCC passed a resolution that Mr J. Sexton Simmonds Chief Officer of the MFB resigns, he refused but was dismissed and departed on July 31st.

On November 3rd Commander Lionel De Latour Wells RN, elected Chief Officer and commenced his duties on November 9th.

New fire engine station opened in Kingsland Road on 30th April, the station at Shoreditch also opened, street stations at Columbia Road, and at Tower Hill, a hose cart at Ridley Road Dalston. Fire Escapes at Richmond Road Dalston, Hyde Road Hoxton, Glyn Road, Lower Road Clapton, Finsbury Market, Church Sreet, Bethnal Green Road, and the watching duty of the newly erected building of the General Post Office, at St. Martins - Le - Grand.

1897; New fire station to be built at Fulham. Steamers added to the following stations, Knightsbridge, Hammersmith, Stoke Newington, Shooters Hill and Clapham. Additionally steamers added to Kingsland Road and New Cross stations. The duty at the new Whitefriars station commenced on 21st July.

February 1898, as one of the results of experience of a recent large fire, arrangements have been made to keep the firemen supplied with refreshments during their work, provision vans are to be provided with the means of supplying hot tea and coffee, so that when the men are engaged in fighting a large fire they may be able to get both food and a suitable drink.

1898 March 1st. Additional steamers placed at White cross Street, Watling Street, Tooley Street and Waterloo Road. Duty with a manual engine commenced at North End Road on the 7ty July and at Lee Green on 18th October.

At a council meeting, Mr Hubbard moved and the council agreed, to put to the Fire Brigade Committee, that men other than seamen should be enrolled into the brigade. At the Fire Brigade Committee meeting, it was proposed to increase the strength of the Brigade by 25 men. The Fire brigade Committee submitted to the LCC a scheme which, while it would involve an outlay immediately of £200,000, it would hope to prove profitable on account of the additional protection it would achieve to property.

The chief points in Commander Wells' proposals were: -

1/   Distribution of men in small stations (at each one should be kept horses), from which they may in case of need be drawn and concentrated wherever required.

2/   Dispensing with certain existing street duties within a radius of ¾ of a mile from a station at which there is a fire escape capable of being drawn by horses.

3/   Keeping two pairs of horses at every station at which a steam fire engine as well as a horsed escape is kept.

The Committee decided to accept the recommendations which, if carried out will mean a capital expenditure estimated at £197,185 and an annual cost for maintenance of £23,179. An expenditure of £152,500, adds one penny to the rates, so that the cost of the proposed improvements, if paid off in one year, would amount to three half pence.

The general recommendations of the committee may be stated as follows.

1/   That the estimate of £197,185 to be submitted to the finance committee in respect of the provision of additional protection from fire in London be approved.

2/   That the council decide that each fire station shall be equipped with at least a steam fire engine, a fire escape drawn by horses, a hose cart and a light manual escape, and that the staff of the station shall consist of one officer, nine firemen and two coachmen with four horses.

3/   The council to decide that each sub - station shall be equipped with at least a fire escape drawn by horses, a hose cart and light manual escape and that the staff of the station shall consist of one officer, nine firemen and two coachmen, with four horses.

4/   That the council approve the principle of dispensing as a rule, with fire escape and hose cart stations within a radius of approximately three - quarters of a mile of a station at which there is a fire escape drawn by horses.

It would appear from the table in the report that a scheme will involve the erection of four full stations, those being at Hampstead, Lee Green, East Greenwich and South Battersea, at a total cost of £58,000, 18 sub - stations at a cost of £133,000 and the provision of eight steam fire engines and twenty-nine horsed escapes at an expenditure of £6,185.

The new sub - stations to be at Charlton, Eltham, Rushey Green, Vauxhall, Camberwell New Road, Herne hill, Penge, Brixton Hill, Roehampton, North End Fulham, Kilburn, Bayswater, Caledonian Road, Highbury, Upper Hollaway, Homerton, Limehouse and Plumstead. (Some of these stations had already been built others were not built).

The general principles which in the opinion of the Chief Officer, should govern fire brigade work in London are as follows; - It should be practicable to concentrate 100 men in under 15 minutes in any dangerous area for large fire occurrences, on any call the firemen ought, if the machine leaves the station at once, to reach the scene of the fire in less than five minutes.

The staff of the Brigade now consists of 867 firemen including the Chief Officer, Second Officer, Superintendents and all ranks, 32 men under instruction, 17 pilots, 77 coachmen, 3 storekeepers and 5 clerks. The Brigade has 59 land fire stations, 5 floating or river stations, 3 sub - stations, 16 street stations, 60 hose cart duties, 11 hose and ladder truck duties, 205 fire escape duties, 8 steam fire engines on barges, 59 land station fire engines, 53 6in manual fire engines, 7 under 6in manual fire engines, 7 hose tenders and escapes, 14 hose and ladder trucks, 115 hose carts, 36 miles of hose, 18 steam tugs, 12 barges, 12 skiffs, 235 fire escape, 5 long fire ladders, 7 ladder vans, 2 trolleys for engines, 11 hose and coal vans, 6 traps for visiting, one stores van, 2 wagons for street duties, 156 watch boxes, 159 horses, 114 telephone lines to police stations, 89 telephone lines to public and other buildings, 9 bell ringing fire alarms to public and other buildings and one speaking tube to a public building.

By December, considerable progress was being made with the equipment of the MFB, with the horse fire escapes, which it has decided to adopt for the metro use as a result of the great Cripplegate fire. Some 29 stations have already been provided with the appliances, a good number of others will shortly have them, as the manufacturers are hard at work upon the councils order.

The practice is to dispatch a steam fire engine after a horse escape on every occasion where the fire engine is in the neighbourhood of the station. If the escape is found not to be wanted it is at once sent back, so that it is usually only absent for a few minutes.

1899; at the meeting of the LCC held on Tuesday May 9th, the Fire Brigade Committee presented an important report on the necessity for a new city fire station in the area of the Cripplegate fire, there are four stations in the city, Bishopsgate, Whitefriars, Watling Street and Whitecross Street. The 1st two are modern the third well placed but inconvenient in every other respect and the last too small.

August 3rd, the station at Lewisham opened.

September, The fire brigade took possession of a large building that had been erected at a cost of £6,000, at the southern end of Battersea Bridge for the accommodation of the men attached to the floating fire appliance stationed at Battersea Bridge. The men had previously lodged at private houses locally. The building consists of 15 suits of rooms for married firemen. The basement is to be used by the LCC for storage purposes.

October, the floating station on the western side of Hungerford, or as it is more generally called Charing Cross Bridge, is about to be demolished, as a new one is being built alongside Blackfriars Bridge at its northern end.

1900 March 1st, Foundation stones laid for new stations in Paddington at Edgware Road, Upper Street Islington, the station in Essex Road will close, and a sub - station erected at Highbury, with sub - station at Holloway.

1900. May 1st, the sanction of the LCC has been asked for the establishment of the Marconi system of wireless telegraphy for fire alarm purposes in Streatham.

It is necessary for the communication to be maintained between the large fire station at Streatham Green and the temporary sub - -station at 45 Mitcham Lane.

An underground telephone apparatus would cost £280. Although the distance is only 400 yards, and it was found impracticable to obtain permission to carry even temporary an overhead wire between the two stations. The Chief officer suggested a trial of wireless telegraphy, and an offer has been made to install and maintain the Marconi system for two years in consideration of an annual payment of £50. It is this offer which the council has been asked to accept. The report of the Fire Brigade Committee states that the experiment will afford an opportunity of ascertaining whether wireless telegraphy can be further adopted for use by the Brigade. In his annual report, the Chief Officer stated that after a long series of experiments, he was satisfied that the land steamers kept at some stations may, with considerable benefit, be worked by oil fuel. For the last six months there has been a steamer worked by the oil fuel standing ready at the Watling Street station and capable of being ready on full steam in two and a half minutes following a call. The speed in which this can be achieved and for other reasons the brigade will pursue the developement of oil.

September, the Islington Fire Station opened at a cost of £20,594, with steamer, horsed escape, hose cart and hand escape, 19 firemen 2 coachmen and five horses. Foundation stone for Red Cross Street laid. Proposals to erect new fire station at Kensington , north side of the High Street, little to the east of the present one in Ball Street. November 22nd, the station at Paddington opened.

1901. March 1st, it has been decided that all horses of the MFB, shall carry a set of a dozen bells, the use of the bells has been left to the discretion of the officer - in - charge at different stations, but now the practice will be for all the stations as 150 dozen bells are in the process of being affixed to leather strips at the Southwark HQ.

April saw Mr J.Gilbert Chairman of the Fire Brigade Committee open the station at Redcross Street, which will replace the station at Whitecross Street, and the new fire station at Uxbridge Road Shepherds Bush. The 1st station cost £31,000 for the site and £13,316 for the building costs; it has a horsed escape, two steam engines, long ladder and hose cart and stables for six horses. The 2nd station cost £12,600 with a steamer and horsed escape, hose cart and a spare horse, accommodation for an officer, 9 firemen, 2 coachmen and four horses.

June, At a recent meeting of the LCC it was decided to purchase an automobile, by the way of an experiment for the use of the inspection branch, and for teaching firemen the method of driving a motor. The cost including spare boiler and tyres will be £286. Monday July 29th, foundation stone laid for new sub - station in Homerton High Street, while on December the 14th the foundation stone was laid at site of the Euston road station.

1902, February 6th station opened at West End Lane near Mill Lane Hampstead. March the fire station at Westcombe Park East Greenwich, opened as a full station, with steam fire engine, horsed escape and 12 firemen, site cost £1.050 and built for £13.100. The station at Perry Vale opened on Saturday March 22nd.

Two firemen were infected with Small - pox when they attended an incident on board a hospital ship on the Thames. New sub - station to be erected at Lothair Road Hornsey, and new fire station at Grafton square Clapham to replace the old station at Old Town, which had been built in 1867, memorial stone was laid on July 12th. September, chairman of the Fire brigade Committee laid foundation stone for the new station at Blackstock Road Highbury. November 1st new full station opened by the vice chair of the Fire brigade Committee Mr Allen at High Street Homerton. A turn - out drill at the new station showed the horsed escape being out in 30 seconds and the engine in 55 seconds. In his opening speech Mr Allen stated that the council intended to increase from four full fire stations that had been proposed under the 1898 scheme to seven full stations.

On the 27th November, Mr Allen Chairman of the Fire Brigade Committee, opened the new fire station at Euston Road at the junction of Drummond Street, cost £7,700 with a horsed escape, steam fire engine and a 70ft ladder, Superintendent Lester in charge and 18 firemen. Mile End station to be rebuilt on existing site.

1903 Saturday February 7th, foundation stone laid for two new stations, one to be built at Vauxhall at the Albert Embankment and the other at Mitcham Lane Streatham, designed to replace street fire stations. Mr Allen performed the stone laying ceremonies and said that this was part of a scheme adopted by the LCC in 1898 for the better protection of London from fire. Mr John Burns MP, stated that the fire brigade had now been doubled and the appliances had been improved beyond recognition.

Since the LCC took over from the MBW, they have increased the horse equipment from 131-294, with 63 horsed escapes, the steam fire engines from 48-78, the sub - stations from 7-19 street fire alarms from 315-813, fire hydrants from 8,881-27,493 and the establishment from 677-1222.

Tuesday March 3rd, foundation stone laid for the Pageants Wharf station in Rotherhithe Street. A new station to be erected at Deptford and one to be built North side of Clarence Mews, Kensington High Street. The new station at Blackstock Road Highbury was opened on April 2nd.

July 27th foundation stone laid for the new station at the Old Kent Road and the new one at Deptford, the Chairman in his speech stated that the council decided to demolish the old Deptford station and replace it with a new one on the site rather than extend the old station.

Saturday October 4th the Chairman of the Fire Brigade Committee opened Vauxhall fire station, built by the LCC works department with an establishment of an officer, 5 firemen and a coachman. The same afternoon the Chairman opened the station built at Pageants Wharf Rotherhithe Street, situated between Surrey Docks and the river with an establishment of an officer 6 firemen and a coachman.

The Fire Brigade Committee at its meeting on November 10th submitted for the approval of the council a report in which they recommend that compulsory powers should be sought in the next session of parliament to acquire sites for new fire stations in place of the Watling Street, Shooters Hill and Knightsbridge fire stations. The total estimated cost of these three fire stations, including site and building is £115,500, comprising £63,500 for the new station in place of the Watling Street station, £12,000 for the Shooters Hill station, £40,000 for the one at Knightsbridge. The premises selected as the site of the new city fire station are no's, 86-88 Queen Victoria Street and no's, 30-32 Cannon Street. Arrangements have already arrived at with the occupying leases of 88 Queen Victoria Street and 30 Cannon Street. It is proposed to keep at the new station a horsed escape, two steam engines and a 70 ft ladder and that it shall be the Superintendents station of the central District. On its opening the Watling Street station will close. With regard to the Knightsbridge station the committee have for some time been impressed with the need of providing a better fire station in the locality than the present one in Chapel Place Relton Mews. The site selected for the new station is at the junction of Hooper's Court with Basil Street immediately opposite Pavilion Road.

The station which will replace the present fire station at the junction of Shooters Hill Road and Woolwich Common Road, will be erected on the plateau at the top of Shooters Hill. It is considered that from a station in this position appliances could be very rapidly drawn to the upper parts of Plumstead, as well as to the large amounts of Government property in the neighborhood of Woolwich Common.

1904 February 25th, Mr E. Smith Chairman of the Fire Brigade Committee, laid the foundation stone at the Maida Vale Kilburn site and at the Pickering Place, Bayswater site. Mr Smith stated that on average a new fire station was opened every two months. On May 14th he opened the new fire station at Deptford, in declaring the station opened he said the one erected on the site in 1869 cost £1,600 but was small and inconvenient. After consideration it was decided to erect an entirely new station at a cost of £10,350 with three cottages being built in the yard. A recreation room with a billiard table had also been provided for the men. The second floor was for the station officers quarters, consisting of four rooms scullery and private bathroom. The third floor contained three bedrooms. The stables contained four stalls, three of which opened directly onto the appliance room and fodder store.

21st July memorial stone laid by Mr Lewin Sharp, vice chairman of the Fire Brigade Committee at Clarence Mews, High Street Kensington. A new station is being built at Burdett Road.

On August 23rd the officers and men of the Brigade were officially notified in orders that, under the provisions of the General Powers Act of the LCC 1904, the title of the organisation is changed from that of the 'Metropolitan Fire Brigade', to that of the 'London Fire Brigade'. The organisation has borne the title of the MFB since its establishment by the now defunct Metropolitan Board of Works.

New fire stations to be built at Shooters Hill and Brockley, the new stations at Westbourne Grove, Bayswater, Old Kent Road and Maida Vale opened and the new station at Pickering Place Bayswater also opened, this station allowed the Paddington Green station to close. At a council meeting the Fire Brigade Committee stated that a new station would be erected to replace the present station in Waterloo Road. Mr Smith opened the new station at Streatham, during the ceremony the firemen had a fire call and they immediately turned out within 30 seconds to a house fire in New Park Road. New sub - station erected at a cost of £8,000 opened in the High Street Eltham.

1905; New fire stations opened at Kensington High Street Northcote Road and at West Ferry Road.

The Chief Officer, Captain Hamilton stated that in order to ensure the prompt attendance of an adequate force of men in response to all calls to fire, he has issued orders for the number of men forming the crew of all horsed escapes in the London Fire brigade to be increased from three to four. December saw the opening of the Wapping station in Red Lion Street, this station being the first supplied with motor traction appliances only.

1906 new station opened on May 22nd at Greycoat Place Westminster. The cost to the council of erecting the station being £24,000. It has a steam fire engine, horsed escape and a long ladder staffed by 17 firemen. Thursday July 26th station at Brixton and Herne Hill opened.

The Brigade now owns the following motor appliances; three fire engines, two escapes, a chassis, a tractor and a horse tender. Two new motor fire engines are on order, in addition, and a horsed engine is being adapted for motor traction. Lee Green Fire Station opened.

1907, the new station which the LCC has erected in the city was formally opened on Wednesday February 21st 1907, though it has exactly similar frontages to both to Cannon Street and Queen Victoria street, it is known as the Cannon Street Fire Station, it will have forty firemen. The street stations at Farringdon Street, The General Post Office and at Fishmongers' Hall will cease. The Fire Station at Watling Street will also close, this old station was formerly a city hotel, kept by two maiden ladies. One night in the late fifties, they were saved from death by the members of the old LFEE. To mark their gratitude they bequeathed the building to them to be used as a fire and fire - escape station. Both James Braidwood and Sir Eyre Massey Shaw had their headquarters there.

In the Chief Officers report for the year 1906, he stated that motor traction for the brigade appliances was rapidly increasing with the new fire station at Lee Green, opened last December, which had been entirely equipped with motor appliances.

The first such station being that at Wapping in Red Lion Street, which opened in the December of 1905. Other stations in the course of construction will be of entirely motor appliances.

New station opened by The Hon. Rupert Guinness, Chairman of the Fire Brigade Committee, on June 20th at High Street Plumstead, and then on June 25th at Calverley Grove, Hornsey Rise, erected at a cost of £8,000.

The Fire Brigade Committee contemplated erecting a new fire station in the Bromley Road Catford, when erected the new building will take the place of the existing sub - station at Rushey Green, which the council hold on a lease. The Chairman opened the new station at Knightsbridge corner of Sloane Street, on the 27th June, the new station replaces a former fire station which was housed in some disused mews.

1908. 27th February, The Hon. Rupert Guinness Chairman of the Fire Brigade Committee, opened the new station at Tooting, the station being entirely up - to - date, all the engines in use are motor engines, one being a motor steamer. This station replaced the old station in Balham High Street. The engine room is the largest of any in London. The turn out switch rings electric bells in every room in the building and lights the electric lights, while in the engine room different coloured electric lights indicate to the firemen as they slide down poles from their apartments or rush from the recreation room the appliance which is ordered. A red light means the escape, a green light means the motor engine and the two in conjunction with the yellow light indicate all the appliances are to be turned out. October the new station at Holloway in Mayton Road was opened, replacing the station that was built in 1871. Sub – station at Charlton opened.

1909. February 4th, work commenced on the extension to the London Fire Brigade Headquarters at Southwark Bridge Road, a new engine house, workshops and apartments for the Divisional Officers and Assistant Officers will be erected. July 20th saw the first motor appliance sub - station of the LCC opened in Copenhagen Street, Caledonian Road Islington. Approval for a new station at Waterloo to replace the existing station, and for alteration to the Woolwich station, which will cost £5,000.

1910 June 23rd both the station at Waterloo Road and at Foxley Road Camberwell were opened. Brunswick Road station opened.

1911 LCC propose a new fire station at Hammersmith and the new station at Shooters Hill will be built at a cost of £11,973. The new Southwark and Bow Stations now completed.

PARTICULARS OF PROSECUTIONS IN CONNECTION WITH THE LONDON FIRE BRIGADE, 1911.

A.—CASES OF ARSON, INCENDIARISM, ETC.

Date.	Where fire occurred.	Nature of charge.	Where charged and date.	Result.
1911. Jan. 7	23, Dumbarton-road, Brixton, S.W.	Wilfully setting fire to premises	Lambeth Police Court, 11th January, 1911	Bound over in the sum of £10 to be of good behaviour for 3 months.
Mar. 5	170, Jamaica-road, Bermondsey, S.E.	Arson	Central Criminal Court, 5th April, 1911	Sentenced to 12 months' hard labour.
Mar. 30	Vernon-place, W.C. ..	Wilfully setting fire to premises	Central Criminal Court, 31st March, 1911.	Discharged.
May 17	Corman-street, King's Cross, N.	Do. do.	South London Sessions, 14th June, 1911	Do.
May 18	5, Normand-road, West Kensington, W.	Do. do.	Central Criminal Court, 17th July, 1911	Certified to be insane, and removed to an asylum.
May 29	175, Euston-road, N.W...	Do. do.	Central Criminal Court, 27th June, 1911	Discharged.
July 25	22, Caledonia-street, Caledonian-road, N.	Murder and wilfully setting fire to premises	Central Criminal Court, 12th September, 1911	Sentenced to death.
Nov. 15	3, Bude-mansions, Charing Cross-road, W.C.	Wilfully setting fire to premises	Central Criminal Court, 11th December, 1911	Discharged.

B.— CASES OF MALICIOUS FALSE ALARMS AND INTERFERENCE WITH FIRE ALARMS.

Date.	Name and position of fire-alarm.	Nature of charge.	Magistrate who heard case.	Result.
1911. Jan. 3	Bethnal Green-junction, Cambridge-road, E.	Wilfully breaking glass of fire-alarm	Mr. A. R. Cluer ..	Discharged, but advised to pay 3d. damage, the cost of the glass (Paid).
Jan. 8	Latchmere-road, at corner of Shellwood-street, Battersea, S.W.	Giving false alarm of fire	Mr. C. K. Francis ..	Discharged owing to insufficient evidence of identification.
Feb. 19	Mortimer-street, at Berner-street, W.	Wilfully breaking glass of fire-alarm	Mr. G. L. Denman ..	Sentenced to 2 months' hard labour.
Mar. 4	Angel-road, at King-street, W.	Giving false alarm of fire	Mr. E. W. Garrett ..	Fined 40s., or in default to undergo 1 month's imprisonment. (Fine not paid)
Mar. 7	Queen-street, at Upper Thames-street, E.C.	Wilfully breaking glass of fire-alarm	Sir Vesey Strong (Lord Mayor)	Sentenced to 1 day's imprisonment.
Mar. 8	City-road, at East-road, E.C.	Giving false alarm of fire	Mr. A. R. Cluer ..	Discharged.
Mar. 17	Stainer-street, at Tooley-street, S.E.	Do. do.	Mr. J. Rose	Fined 40s., or in default to undergo 14 days' imprisonment. (Fine not paid.)
April 2	Hermitage-road, at Green-lanes, N.	Wilfully breaking glass of fire-alarm	Mr. T. C. Hedderwick	Fined £1 and 2d. damage. (Fine paid.)
April 3	Burdett-road, at Thomas-street, E.	Giving false alarm of fire	Mr. J. Dickinson ..	Bound over in his own recognisance of £5 to be of good behaviour for 2 years.
April 18	Follywall, at Manchester-road, E.	Wilfully breaking glass of fire-alarm	Mr. Chester Jones ..	Fined 5s. and 10s. costs and 3d. damage. (Fine paid.)
April 23	Cow-lane, at Rotherhithe-street, S.E.	Giving a false alarm of fire	Mr. Cecil Chapman ..	Fined £2 and 10s. costs. (Fine paid.)
May 3	Rhodeswell-road, at St. Paul's-road, E.	Do. do.	Mr. Chester Jones ..	Fined 40s. and 3d. damage, or in default to undergo 1 month's imprisonment. (Fine not paid.)
May 9	Macklin-street, at Drury-lane, W.C.	Do. do.	Mr. R. H. B. Marsham	Fined £20, or in default to undergo 2 months' imprisonment. (Fine not paid.)
May 10	Glenforth-street, at Glenister-road, S.E.	Do. do.	Mr. A. H. Hutton ..	Fined £2, or in default to undergo 7 days' imprisonment. (Fine not paid.)
June 5	Clarendon-square, at Phœnix-street, N.W.	Wilfully breaking glass of fire-alarm	Mr. J. R. W. Bros ..	Bound over in the sum of £2 to be of good behaviour for 12 months.

1912 The new station in Eaglesfield Road, Shrewsbury Lane, built to replace the one in Shooters Hill Road, was opened on the 7th of October by the Chairman of the Committee Mr. J. B. Karslake. The station is entirely equipped with motor fire appliances.

To accelerate the turn - out, considerable structural alterations were carried out at the Whitefriars and Islington fire stations, and sliding poles fitted at the Perry Vale, Edgware Road, Shoreditch, Shadwell, Dulwich, Fulham and Homerton stations.

The reconstruction of the East and North East Blocks at Headquarters and the installation of a second underground store for containing petrol in bulk was completed. A rifle range was also provided. These were opened on the 18th December last, by the Chairman of the Council, Major General The Right Hon. Lord Cheylesmore, K.C.V.O,. D.L..

Motor Escape Vans have now been provided at Headquarters, Westminster, Brompton, North End Road, Hornsey Rise, Eltham, Herne Hill, Old Kent Road and Cannon Street fire stations and the horsed escapes withdrawn. Petrol motor fire engines have been substituted for steam motor or horsed fire engines at the Wapping, Whitechapel, New Cross, Clapham, Kensington and Hammersmith fire stations. The placing of a motor escape van at the Brompton station will make it no longer necessary to retain the one at Battersea River station.

Electric light has been installed at the Dulwich, Greenwich, North Kensington, Stoke Newington, and Hampstead fire stations. Facilities for carrying out hook ladder drills have been provided at the West Hampstead, Bishopsgate, Bethnal Green, Homerton and East Greenwich fire stations. The system of synchronising the clocks in the public rooms at fire stations has been further extended to certain clocks at the Clapham, Edgware Road, Whitefriars and Kilburn stations.

Ten pairs of smoke helmets of the self - contained type have been purchased so as to ensure that such apparatus will be available without delay in any part of London.

1913. The Chief officer in his annual report to the council, stated that of the 94 fatal fires of the past year 26 were due to children playing with fire or matches, 27 were caused by persons' clothing coming into contact with fire or gas - stoves, 10 were caused by sparks from fires and 8 were the result of mineral oil lamps being upset or exploding.

The lives of 148 persons were endangered at fires, of these 43 were rescued by members of the Brigade with the aid of fire appliances, or were assisted out by firemen, the remainder making their escape by other means. In addition to the 3,377 fires, 645 were chimney fires.

By 31st December 1913, there were 1,554 (including 6 private) street fire - alarms which rang into 84 fire stations. A card index of fire - alarms in place of the fire - alarm books normally used at fire stations was placed in operation during the year.

The number of false alarms received was 1,798. The number of malicious false alarms continued to rise, the highest recorded, 436, compared with 425 in the previous year. There were 39 persons prosecuted for maliciously calling the brigade or interfering with the alarms. With a view to reducing the number of malicious false alarms received, the Council decided to offer a reward of £1 to the person or persons, other than the police, who give information resulting in the conviction of a person giving a malicious false alarm.

In connection with calls received through the telephone exchanges, complaints are from time to time made as to the delay of the Fire Brigade. This generally arises through the person calling omitting to give the address of the fire or not waiting at the instrument until direct connection to the fire station is established.

The number of fire hydrants in London is 28,911. The Brigade made 177,582 hydrant inspections and 177,414 inspections of hydrant indicator tablets. Special indicating plates have been fitted adjacent to the councils' double hydrants in order to distinguish these hydrants from those of single outlets. Similar tablets have been fixed adjacent to all the double hydrants in the City of London, the latter hydrants are the property of the Corporation of London. An underground water tank to serve as a supply for fire engines has been installed in Pepys Road, New Cross S.E. This is the first tank of the kind provided by the Council and fixed in the streets of London.

The reconstruction of the Hackney and Hammersmith fire stations is practically complete, and similar work is in progress at the New Cross and Clerkenwell fire stations.

With a view to adapting the buildings for motor appliances and accelerating the turnout, various improvements, including sliding poles in some instances, have been completed, or in hand, at the North Kensington, Stoke Newington, Shadwell, Dulwich, Lewisham and Streatham fire stations.

A gymnasium has been erected at the Northcote Road station, it was opened on the 26th November by Mr Fred H. Carter Chairman of the LCC Fire Brigade Committee, costing £1. 500 the gymnasium is the first of its kind in the brigade to be provided in connection with a district fire station, and one is also being constructed at the New Cross and Bishopsgate stations. Electric light has been installed at the Hampstead station, to provide better facilities for carrying out hook ladder drill, the drill towers at Whitechapel and Mile End Road stations have been reconstructed.

During the year there had been added to the Brigade equipment seven petrol - driven motor fire engines, five petrol - driven motor (escape) vans, one electrically - driven motor turntable ladder, one electrically- driven motor chassis for a turntable ladder conversion, one petrol - driven motor lorry and three petrol - driven motor cars for officers.

Motor escape vans, in substitution for horsed escape vans, have been supplied to the North Kensington, Hammersmith, Clerkenwell, Hackney, New Cross and Perry Vale fire stations. Petrol - driven motor fire engines have replaced horsed steam fire engines at the North Kensington, Clerkenwell, Hackney and Perry Vale fire stations. Electrically - driven motor turntable ladders have replaced horsed long ladders at Headquarters and Westminster fire stations. A petrol - driven motor lorry has been placed at the Clerkenwell station.

Motor cars in place of horse - drawn visiting traps have been placed at the Clerkenwell and Whitefriars stations.

Following the deaths of two firemen from asphyxiation by gas in a sewer, the efficiency of the self - contained smoke helmets has cause for concern by the Brigade. The practice of carrying the apparatus in pairs on appliances and training a few men at each of the thirteen stations that are equipped with the smoke helmets will cease with the removal of them from appliances. It has been decided to purchase two new specially fitted appliances for smoke helmets, one already being built and will be placed at Headquarters, and will have specially trained firemen for these appliances.

There will however be kept at nineteen fire stations smoke helmets of a simpler and less expensive type for use pending the arrival of the special appliance.

1914. The chief Officer in his report to the Council for the year 1914, stated that contrary to what might have been anticipated, the war had no appreciable effect on either the number or nature and extent of fire in London. The contingency of the depletion of the strength of the brigade by so many men on the outbreak of hostilities was met by withdrawing certain sub - stations, street - stations and other out - duties previously arranged for on delivery of motor appliances, readjusting the staff at various other stations and discontinuing instructional classes. These arrangements were completed about the end of September, since when the conditions in the Brigade have been practically normal.

Consequently upon the absence of the men called up with the Royal Fleet and Army reserves, the remaining men in the Brigade had to carry out a large amount of extra work and most of them had to forgo their annual leave. The Council granted each of the officers and men, below the rank of assistant divisional officer, a week's pay, which was paid in Christmas week. Considerable difficulty was experienced in recruiting men for the Brigade during the war and, to overcome this problem the Council decided to establish a rank of temporary' fireman.

The North End Road, Chelsea and Battersea Park Road sub - stations were closed.

The Hammersmith and Hackney stations following reconstruction were officially opened by Mr . Percy C. Simmons, LCC the Chairman of the Fire Brigade Committee.

Various improvements including allowing for the change over to motor appliances and a faster turn out, have been made at the Westminster, Shepherd's Bush, Islington, East Greenwich and Old Kent Road stations.

At the Pageant's Wharf sub - station two 50 ton oil tanks have been installed, together with the necessary pumps, boiler and fittings. The oil is for the use of the fire float "Beta II." Again more motor appliances have been added to the Brigade fleet to replace horse drawn appliances. The war delayed the arrival of some motor appliances ordered; of the twelve motor pumps and similar number of motor escape vans, only two of each type had so far been received. So far motor pumps, motor escape vans or motor ladders have replaced horse drawn appliances at Headquarters, Brompton, Euston, Red Cross Street, Whitechapel, Dulwich, Lewisham and Old Kent Road. Following their replacement their are now several horse drawn appliances, steam fire engines, fire escapes, vans etc, for disposal. A new emergency tender has been placed into service, it carries a number of smoke helmets and is fitted with a dynamo, portable searchlights and an electric blower for forcing air into places where dense smoke or poisonous gases exist. It is manned by specially selected and trained men who devote their time to maintaining the equipment. The LCC decided to undertake extensive modernising alterations to the Kennington fire station. It is proposed to enlarge the appliance room and to carry out alterations necessary to adapt the station for equipment with motor appliances and to build a full size recreation room in the yard. All the married men's quarters will have three rooms and will be self - contained and a cubicle will be provided for each of the single men on the strength of the station. The preliminary cost of the work is £11,000.

Workshops, the volume of repair work undertaken by the Brigade workshops has increased and additional room is required. A larger permanent extension is required, but in the meantime in order to cope with the work a temporary building is to be built. In 1902 when motor appliances were first adopted in the Brigade, the staff of the workshops consisted of a mechanical engineer, a clerk and 39 mechanics and labourers, the establishment of the workshops now comprises of, 1 mechanical engineer, 5 technical and clerical assistants, 1 foreman, 1 deputy foreman and 67 mechanics and labourers.

Inspection work, of over 1,280 buildings, etc, are regularly inspected by staff detailed for this work, these include Government and national buildings, theatres and music halls, cinematograph halls, public entertainment halls, restaurants and public rooms in hotels, licensed lodging houses and buildings of large cubical extent sanctioned by the Council under section 17 and 18 of the General Powers Act, 1908. The arrangements of large public exhibitions (including those held at Earl's Court and the White City) and the fire protective arrangements of the seven tube railways are also periodically inspected.

1915. Following the conversion of the Bayswater station into a full station and the equipment of two neighbouring stations with motor appliances, the Notting Hill fire station was closed. The Council decided on the 20th & 27th July 1915, that the undermentioned street stations should be discontinued as soon as neighbouring fire station were equipped with motor appliances and a fire - alarm post had been fixed at or near the site of the street station Haymarket, St. James's Place (Houndsditch), and Bartholomew Close (City). During the year Belsize opened.

Owing to the war, it was decided on 13th July 1915, to postpone the extension of Euston station, the erection of a new station in substitution for Tooley Street station, and the enlargement of Kennington station.

On 28th October 1915, it was decided to postpone the erection of a hose - hoist and drill tower at Kentish Town station, and the provision of facilities for hook - ladder drill at Holloway station.

The new temporary workshops had been opened during the year giving the much needed space for repair work to the Brigades appliances.

1916. During the year no work done at or to any fire station in the Brigade. The capital received air raids during August, September and in November the estimated monetary loss was put at £196,147.

The work of the inspection section was further effected by the war with staff enlisting into H.M. forces. Women were enlisted to help by doing the clerical work, while technical officers were temporarily replaced by officers from other departments. New station at West Norwood built to replace the station built in 1882 in the High street.

1917; The West Ham Fire Brigade on 19th January 1917, was called at 6:45 pm, to a fire on the premises of Messrs. Brunner, Mond and Co., Ltd, North Woolwich, Silvertown, Whilst the men and appliances from their Silvertown station were getting to work, a terrific explosion occurred at about 6:50 pm. This killed two firemen and severely injured five others. The casualties and damage done by the explosion was widespread, and several very serious fires were started. Due to damaged communications, the London Fire Brigade was not called until 7:29pm. The London Fire Brigade was already responding to calls to fires started by the explosion including a gasometer involved at the Metropolitan Gas Works at Blackwall. The Brigade employed over 50 motor fire pumps from the Friday to the Monday morning.

1918. On 24th February, Mr Gamble Divisional Officer, retired on the grounds of ill - health, and on the 31st December 1918 Commander Sladen, Chief Officer resigned. Mr AR. Dyer who was then the senior divisional officer, was appointed acting Chief Officer from 1st January 1919. After other applications for the position had been considered he was promoted on 3rd June 1919, Chief Officer of the London Fire Brigade and the London Ambulance Service.

At a fire which occurred in the early hours of 30th January 1918, at the Albert Embankment, Lambeth, Sub Officer WE. Cornford, Sub Officer WW. Hall, Firemen EJ. Fairbrother, JWC. Johnson, AA. Page, and WE. Nash, and temporary Fireman JE. Fay were killed, and Supt, J. Barrows and Stn O. E. Partner injured. The fire was on the two upper floors of a building of three floors used as a manufactory for cattle food. The loss of life, one of the heaviest in the history of the Brigade, was due to the collapse of the building.

During the period of 1918, the "representative body" of the Brigade put forward to the council that following the ending of the war with Germany, that the shift system of an eight hour day should be established.

The council considered the proposal and on the 22nd July 1919, decided not to approve the request, the proposal being put forward to a tribunal. In the council report to the tribunal, it stated that it had made a compromise in the autumn of 1919, to establish a non - residential shift system on the basis of two shifts of twelve hours a day, or the equivalent during the summer of 1920, on the understanding that the "representative body" undertook not to apply for a forty eight hour week until 28th June 1922. It was hoped, upon a more thorough examination of the organization of the Brigade, which by the adoption of the scheme, would undergo drastic alterations, simplified however by the process of motorisation, that it might be possible to close certain fire stations. The Council also decided that the arrangements for which the staff below the rank of Station Officer were required to live in fire stations, should be discontinued, and that as from the introduction of the system at separate stations Sub Officers and permanent firemen should be granted an allowance of 8s 6d. a week each. These men were to be permitted to live out, or where possible and approved by the council to live on some station premises in approved accommodation.

1919. Stations, Appliances, Etc., of The London Fire Brigade.

Land fire stations	79	Motor fire floats	2
floating or river stations	3	store barges	4
river repairing depot	1	skiffs	7
petrol motor fire engines	87	fire escapes	157
petrol motor emergency tender	1	long fire ladders	5
petrol motor tenders	6	horsed turntable long fire ladder	3
petrol motor lorries	2	smoke helmets	36
electric motor escape vans	11	cellar pipes	3
electric motor ladders	4	hook ladders	316
petrol - electric motor ladders	2	hook belts	314
petrol - electric lorries	2	canteen van	1
motor cars	1	watch boxes	3
6in. manual fire engine	1	hose miles of	77
hose carts	86	horses	12
steam fire floats	2	street fire alarms (including 1610 five private alarms).	

1921, The LSC handed over the Shaftsbury Avenue station to the LFB, it will be fitted out as a West End station. On opening, this station will take the place of those stations at Gt. Marlborough Street, Scotland Yard and Holborn all which will close.

24th November saw the last horse drawn escape turnout. Major Percy Simmons, Chairman of the LCC, placed a call at the Kensington fire station, photos and a film record of the event were taken.

1922. The extension to Euston fire station, postponed during the war, was commenced, the erection of a new station to replace that at Tooley street was again deferred due to not finding a suitable site.

Work to adapt the former London Salvage Corps Station in Shafstbury Avenue was completed and the duty commenced on May 10th.

The Kennington, Kilburn, New Scotland Yard and Northcote Road fire stations, which the council on the 23rd March 1920 and 9th November 1920, decided to close, were entirely vacated during the year, and the properties, being surplus to fire brigade requirements, were transferred to the control of the Improvements Committee for disposal. 8th May the station at Gt Marlborough Street closed and the men and appliances transferred to the Shaftsbury Avenue station.

1923. Following the enlargement of the Euston fire station, the station at Holborn closed on the 22 February. The Peckham Road fire station built in 1867 and enlarged in 1881, was now inadequate for modern requirements, and the Council on the 24th July 1923, decided to build a new station in the locality.

The Hampstead, Herne Hill, Highbury, Holborn, Hornsey and Wapping stations which the Council on the 23rd March and 9th November 1920, decided to close, were entirely vacated during the year.

Since the introduction in 1920 of the non - residential shift system, parts of the accommodation at 60 of the present fire stations are no longer required for brigade purposes. Consideration has been given during the year to the question of separating this surplus accommodation from the active portions with a view to the former being disposed of. owing to the expenditure involved, it is proposed in the near future to deal with only twenty stations, which, being situated in the more central districts, are deemed to possess high value for commercial or office purposes and to be likely to recoup the Council outlay.

1925: Peckham station opened replacing the nearby station.

Due to rapid change over the years to better equipment and the gradual change from horse to motor driven engines plus the new shift system, it eventually became possible to close 15 fire stations and still provide the required fire cover as laid down by law.

1927. Dockhead fire station is now being erected and following the opening the stations at Tooley Street and at Rotherhithe will be closed.

1928. 18th October, the duty at the new station at Dockhead commenced, staffed by a Station officer and 34 Sub Officers and Firemen with a motor escape and two motor pumps. The opening of this station allowed the closure of both Tooley Street and Rotherhithe Stations.

1931. The new Whitechapel station opened in Commercial Road.

1932, the new Sub - Station at Downham was completed and opened on the 9th November, this new Sub - Station was staffed by two Sub officers and four Firemen with a motor escape, it appears that since 1928 there had not been any station building or any closures.

1934 saw the next changes in the Brigade when the Fire Brigade Committee on 22nd March, approved the erection of a new Fire Brigade Headquarters on a site purchased by the Council at Albert Embankment, Lambeth. 11th December the Fire Brigade Committee approved the reorganization of the Brigade, resulting in improved appliance design, being the dual purpose appliance with 50ft wheeled metal escape ladders and pumps with 45ft ladders and 10 to carry breathing apparatus sets. Key stations for dual purpose appliances and the rebuilding of certain stations.

The LCC decided that a new station should be built to replace the Cherry Garden Float station and the Pageant's Wharf station.

During the year a fireman and his family were all found dead in their quarters at the Vauxhall fire station. It was found that a gas leak under the road, which had leaked into an open window, was the tragic cause.

1935, 5th March the Council approved the proposals for the erection of buildings on the Albert Embankment at an estimated cost of £279,000.

The new building will be divided into two blocks. The main block of ten floors and basement covering an area 210 ft x 47 ft, the ground floor consisting of a seven bay appliance room, watchroom, breathing apparatus room, control room, gymnasium and canteen, first floor station personnel accommodation and offices, second floor administration section, large conference room and offices for the Chief Officer, senior officers, district officers and sub - officers. Third floor for the general administration, typists, records, waiting room and station officers, fourth floor to be the residential quarters for the Chief Officer and senior officers. Fifth floor will be the residential quarters for the senior District Officer and two station officers. The sixth floor for the residential ADO south, District Officer and Station officer, Seventh floor for the residential ADO attached to Headquarters and two station officers and on the eighth floor residential quarters for two Station officers. Access from the above floors for fire calls will be via four sliding poles into the appliance room. A Brigade museum will also be located within the building with a memorial to those of the Brigade that have lost their lives in the course of their duty in the entrance hall. To the rear of this block will be balconies at the first, second and third floor levels for 800 people to watch the weekly Brigade drills held in the drill yard, the yard being 230 ft x 110 ft. Placed in one corner of the yard will be a drill tower 100ft high of eight storeys with a smoke chamber, this will also be used by recruits and to house wet hose. At the opposite end of the yard will be built a band stand.

The rear block will be of four floors and will be for the training school, with lecture rooms and to accommodate appliances and brigade cars and residential quarters. Behind this building will be the brigade workshops, partly of two floors covering an area of 43,000 sq. ft.

A pontoon and brow will also be erected so as to allow a fireboat to be attached to the HQ.

The tender of Gee, Walker & Slater, Limited of £14,825, was accepted by the council in May of 1935, for the construction of the raft foundations of the main building with the work completed in that year.

October the tenders from twelve companies were received for the erection of the main steel work of the building and the tender of Archibald Dawnay & Sons, Limited, was accepted at a cost of £20,688 10s 4d. Both of the contracts provided that all the materials were supplied wholly by British Empire origin or manufacture.

Battersea Fire Station in Simpson Street, now being the oldest in the Brigade, built in, 1874 and enlarged and improved in 1898, has now become out of date and not suitable for to-days firemen. A new building is proposed on land purchased in Este Road Battersea, the council approving the estimated cost of building being £17,080. The station will be of three bays, with accommodation for 32 men and Sub Officers, with a suite of rooms for the residential Station officer.

November of 1935 saw the closure of the fire station at North Woolwich, a sub station with one motor escape and manned by two firemen. An agreement with the brigade of West Ham Fire Brigade to maintain the fire cover of the area of North Woolwich in return for giving free of charge any support required by the West Ham Brigade.

1936, The Council on 17th March, decided to rebuild Shadwell Station, which had been built in 1881 and had become outdated. A site at 290 Cable Street, corner of Bewley Street has been purchased by the Council for the erection of a new station. This station will be of three turn out bays, with accommodation for 32 Sub Officers and men along with a suite of rooms for a Station officer.

The Charing Cross float repair depot was closed on 2nd October, the pontoon from the depot being adapted for use as a pier at the Albert Embankment river station.

The Council surrendered a strip of land outside Dockhead Station for use as pavement, the Council also acquired land adjacent to Whitechapel Station to extend the drill yard.

Alterations to several stations during the year had also been authorised, formation of additional appliance room both at Brixton and Streatham stations, repaving of appliance room to East Greenwich, widening of appliance room doors at, North Kensington, Stoke Newington and Woolwich, addition of smoke chamber at East Greenwich and Whitechapel, enlargement to drill yard at Kensington, and improvements for storage accommodation at Clapham, East Greenwich and Westminster; improvements also to the officers' and shift accommodation at Brixton, Manchester Square, Plumstead, Streatham, Westminster, West Hampstead and Woolwich.

1937. April saw the partial occupation of the new Fire station at Albert Embankment with the Headquarters being transferred from Southwark in the May, followed soon after by the completion of the pontoon for the fireboat. August saw the Workshops and Training School occupied in the rear block. The work still remaining being to the railway arches for storage and additional workshops and to the band room.

21st July 1937 the official opening of the new headquarters performed by His Majesty the King with Her Majesty the Queen. Display of fire drills and rescue work of the brigade were shown in the drill yard along with a turn out from the appliance bays.

With the opening of the new fire station, Waterloo Road and Vauxhall stations closed as well as the river station at Battersea. Alteration to the following stations approved during the year, improvements to the Station Officers' quarters at Camden Town, re-wiring at Euston, additional toilets and storage room at Stoke Newington and new cycle and hose stores and heating improvements at West Norwood.

1940, April at HQ new underground fire control room opened, constructed to withstand a direct hit from a high explosive bomb and also to render ineffective an attack by poison gas. Built with its own reserve electric light installation and forced ventilation. Above ground is a tapering tower which is designed to pierce any debris from any building that might fall upon it, and is also an emergency escape exit from the control room.

Not until the Second World war did the fire brigade see a major change , that of the The National Fire Service. This was formed by the Government in 1941 to bring together all the brigades of London and around the capital into one force. In charge of the London region was A. N Firebrace the then Chief Officer of the London Fire Brigade. After the war and six and a half years after the NFS was formed, The Fire Service Act of 1947 placed the responsibility of maintaining a fire brigade with County Councils and County Borough Councils.

1948, 31st of March was the last day of the National Fire Service.

1st April and the LCC take over the running of the LFB again with the Chief officer being FW Delve who had been the NFS Regional Fire Officer for London, a new 4 division structure and station identity with a two watch (red & blue), 60 hour week was introduced and so began the task of rebuilding the stations damaged during the war years, although this was not commenced immediately.

1958, The new fire station built at Wandsworth to replace the previously severely war damaged station and the temporary one built in its place, was opened in April by Sir Richard Coppock, CBE., the chairman of the LCC Fire Brigade Committee. During his speech he stated that the LCC had intended to build ten new stations by now but with the problem of housing and rehabilitation so great they were given priority instead. Once the temporary station built in 1955 as a one appliance station had been demolished a new tower would be built. This new station is also the first built to accommodate an AFS appliance and crews.

1959, the Greenwich station opened at Blisset Street, replacing the former station at Grove Street / Lindsell Street, which had been damaged during the war, with the drill yard at the rear being built on the site of the former other station.

1963, Clapham fire station rebuilt on existing site and designed as divisional HQ.

1964 , new station built at Shoreditch again built as a Divisional HQ, transfered from the Clerkenwell station. The station at Whitefriars closed.

1965, New stations at Barbican replacing Redcross street and Bishopsgate and Chelsea built to replace Brompton FS.

1965 also saw a major change for the London Fire Brigade, when the boundaries of the London County Council were enlarged the LCC abolished and the new Greater London Council (GLC) formed. The GLC took over the running of the LFB and all the fire stations that fell within the area. Kent, Surrey, Essex, and Herts all passed over fire stations equipment and some personnel while Middlesex, Croydon, East and West Ham Fire Brigades passed all of their stations and all administration to London.

Next Page: Map of the County of London Lcc c 1953 LFB.

COUNTY OF LONDON
SHOWING FIRE BOUNDARIES

CODE

COUNTY BOUNDARY	
DIVISIONAL FIRE BOUNDARIES	
FIRE STATION BOUNDARIES	
FIRE HEADQUARTERS	
DIVISIONAL FIRE STATIONS	
FIRE STATIONS	

COUNTY OF LONDON COVERED UNDER MUTUAL
ASSISTANCE SCHEME

A CHARING CROSS BR
B WATERLOO BRIDGE
C BLACKFRIARS BR
D BLACKFRIARS BRIDGE
E SOUTHWARK BRIDGE
F CANNON STREET BR
G LONDON BRIDGE
H TOWER BRIDGE

AJN 2004

PLUMSTEAD
C 48

A 20
WOOLWICH

C 44
WOOLWICH

C 47
SHOOTERS HILL

C 49
ELTHAM

C 43
EAST GREENWICH

C 48
LEE GREEN

C 51
DOWNHAM

C 46
GREENWICH

C 50
LEWISHAM

B 28
BRUNSWICK ROAD

MILLWALL
B 34

BLACKWALL TUNNEL

B 26
BOW

B 29
BURDETT ROAD

C 42
DEPTFORD

C 52
PERRY VALE

HOMERTON
B 24

BETHNAL GREEN
B 25

C 41
PAGEANTS WHARF

SOUTHWARK

B 31
SHADWELL

ROTHERHITHE TUNNEL

C 40
NEW CROSS

STOKE NEWINGTON
B 22

KINGSLAND ROAD
B 23

SHOREDITCH
B 27

B 30
WHITECHAPEL

H

D 53
DOCKHEAD

D 54
OLD KENT ROAD

D 55
PECKHAM

B

ISLINGTON
B 21

CLERKENWELL

B 20

RED CROSS STREET
B 33

CANNON ST

WHITEFRIARS

D 62
SOUTHWARK

D 56
BRIXTON

NORWOOD
D 57

HOLLOWAY
B 37

KENTISH TOWN
A 2

CAMDEN TOWN
A 3

A 4
EUSTON

A 5
SOHO

WESTMINSTER BRIDGE

LAMBETH
A 6 HQ

D 51

A BELSIZE
A 15

A 1
MANCHESTER SQUARE

KNIGHTSBRIDGE
A 7

VAUXHALL BRIDGE

CLAPHAM
D 59

STREATHAM
D 58

WEST HAMPSTEAD
A 14

EDGWARE ROAD
A 13

KENSINGTON
A 10

A 8
BROMPTON

BATTERSEA
D 71

TOOTING
D 60

NORTH KENSINGTON
A 12

HAMMERSMITH
A 11

A 9
FULHAM

D 70

WANDSWORTH

PUTNEY BRIDGE

Manchester Square

B1889
altered 1910

c1908
Station No. 2
A district
1 – steam fire engine
1 – horsed escape
1 – horsed long ladder
1 – manual escape
1 – hose cart
1 – manual engine
1 – hose & coal van
1 - trap
1 – Superintendent
1 – District Officer
22 – Firemen
3 – Coachmen
3 – pairs of horses

c1965
Station No. A21
A divisional HQ
Northern Command.

1 – pump escape
1 – pump
1 – turntable ladder
1 – Bacv
1 – Station Officer
1 – Sub Officer
2 – Leading Firemen
19 – Firemen

c2005
Station No. G47
Western Command

1 – pump ladder
1 – pump
1 – Station Officer
1 – Sub Officer
1 – Leading Firefighter
10 – Firefighters

Bethnal Green

B1889
c1908
Station No. 30
C district

1 – steam fire engine
1 – horsed manual
1 – hose cart
1 – Station Officer
11 - Firemen
2 - Coachmen
2 – pairs of horses

c1965
Station No. F26
F Division
Eastern Command

1 – pump escape
1 – pump
1 – Station Officer
1 – Sub Officer
1 – Leading Fireman
11 – Firemen

Wandsworth

B1891
c1908
Station No. E88
E district

1 – steam fire engine
1 – horsed escape
1 – manual escape
1 – hose cart
1 – Station Officer
11 – firemen
2 – Coachmen
2 – pairs of horses

Brompton

B1892
c1908
Station No. A6
A district

1 – steam fire engine
1 – horsed escape
1 – long ladder
1 – hose cart
1 – Station Officer
9 – Firemen
2 – coachmen
2 – pairs of horses

Dulwich

B1892
Station No. D47
D district.

c1908

1 – steam fire engine
1 – horsed escape
1 – manual escape
1 – hose cart
1 – Station Officer
10 – Firemen
2 – coachmen
2 – pairs of horses

New Cross

B1893
Station No. D40
D district

c1908
1 – steam fire engine
1 – horsed escape
1 – horsed long ladder
1 – manual escape
1 – hose cart
1 – hose & coal van
1 – Trap
1 Superintendent
1 District officer
17 Firemen
4 coachmen
3 pairs of horses

c1965
Station No. B29
B division
Southern Command
1 – Pump Escape
1 – Pump
1 – Turntable Ladder
1 - Station Officer
1 - Sub – Officer
2 - Leading Firemen
14 – Firemen

c2005
Station No. E38
Southern Command

1 – pump ladder
1 – Sub Officer
1 – Leading Firefighter
5 - Firefighters

New Cross photo

c1913

with new front to appliance bays with the addition of a third appliance bay.

Rotherhithe river station

Cherry Garden Street SE.

D district station.
B1893

c1908
1 – fire float
1 – store barge
1 – manual escape
1 – Station Officer
16 – Firemen
5 – Pilots

c1913
1 – fire – float
1 – tug
1 – engine on raft
1 – store barge
1 – manual escape

Battersea Sub-Station

Adapted building

C1895
32 Battersea park
Road.
Station No. E91
E district.

c1908
1- hose & ladder truck
3 – Firemen

Kennington

Enlarged & altered
1895/6
Station No. E87
E district

c1903
1 – steam fire engine
1 – horsed escape
1 – horsed long ladder
1 – manual escape
1 – hose cart
1 – motor car
1 – hose & coal tender
1 – hose tender
1 – Assistant
Divisional Officer
1 – Station Officer
17 – Firemen
6 – Coachmen
3 – pairs of horses

Kingsland Road

B1895
Station No. C38
C district.
c1908
1 – steam fire engine
1 – horsed escape
1 – horsed long ladder
1 – manual escape
1 – hose cart
1 – canteen van
1 – Station Officer
16 – Firemen
6 – Coachmen
3 – pairs of horses

c1965
Station No C22
C division Eastern
Command.
1 – pump escape
1 – pump
1 – turntable ladder
1 – Station Officer
1 – Sub Officer
2 – Leading Firemen
14 - Firemen

Kingsland Road

Front of station altered
possibly c1913 to
include third appliance
bay.

Fulham

B1895
Station No. A7
A district

c1908
1 – steam fire engine
1 – horsed escape
1 – horsed long ladder
1 – manual escape
1 – hose cart
1 – Station Officer
13 – Firemen
3 – Coachmen
3 – pairs of horses

c1965
Station No. D24
D division
Northern Command
1 – pump escape
1 – pump
1 – Station officer
1 – Sub Officer
1 – Leading Fireman
11 – Firemen

c2005
Station No. G35
Western Command

Station Commander
1 – pump ladder
1 – pump
1 – Station Officer
1 – Sub Officer
1 – Leading Firefighter
10 - Firefighters

Fulham Escape Shed

adapted building 233 North End Road. Duty commenced 1898.

C1908
1 – horsed escape
1 – manual escape
1 – hose cart
1 – Station Officer
5 – Firemen
2 – Coachmen
1 – pair of horses

Fulham North End Road (sub station)

Shoreditch

B1895
Station No. C37
C district

c1908
2 – steam fire engines
1 – horsed escape
1 – long ladder
1 – hose cart
1 – Station Officer
16 – Firemen
2 – Coachmen
2 – pairs of horses

Clerkenwell

station after alteration
c1896

Clerkenwell

side view of original
station B1870; note the
brickwork is the same
as that in the photo
above beside the
extension of 1896

Clerkenwell

c1908
Station No. B66
B district.
1 – steam fire engine
1 – horsed escape
1 – manual escape
1 – long ladder
1 – hose cart
1 – hose and coal van
1 – trap
1 – Superintendent
1 – District Officer
23 – Firemen
3 – Coachmen
3 – pairs of horses

c1965
Station No. C27
C division
Eastern Command
1 – pump escape
1 – pump
1 – Station Officer
1 – Sub Officer
1 – Leading Fireman
11 – Firemen

c2005
Station No. F47
Eastern Command
1 – pump ladder
1 - pump
1 - Station Officer
1 – Sub Officer
1 – Leading Firefighter
10 – Firefighters

Lee Green Sub Station

Adapted building
c1895
Station No. D45
D district

c1901
1 – horsed escape
1 – manual escape
1 – hose cart
1 – Station Officer
5 – Firemen
2 – Coachmen
1 – pair of horses

Whitefriars

B1896
Station No. F62
F district

c1908
2 – steam fire engines
1 – horsed escape
1 – horsed long ladder
1 – manual escape
1 – hose cart
1 – hose and coal van
Superintendent
1 – District Officer
26 – Firemen
4 – Coachmen
3 – pairs of horses

Lewisham

B1898
Station No. D46
D district.

C1908
1 – steam fire engine
1 – horsed escape
1 – manual escape
1 – hose cart
1 – Station Officer
11 – Firemen
2 – Coachmen
2 – pairs of horses

North Woolwich

B1898
Station No. D51
D district

C1908
1 – hose and ladder
truck
3 – Firemen

Battersea River Station

B1898
Station No. E (river)

c1908
1 – tug
2 – engines on rafts
1 – store barge
1 – motor escape
1 – manual escape
1 – hose cart
1 – Station Officer
11 – Firemen
3 – pilots

Edgware Road

B1899
Station No. A11
A district

c1908
1 – steam fire engine
1 – horsed escape
1 – manual escape
1 – hose cart
1 – Station Officer
11 – Firemen
2 – Coachmen
2 – pairs of horses

c1965
Station No. A30
A division
Northern Command

1 – pump escape
1 – pump
1 – Station Officer
1 – Sub Officer
1 – Leading Fireman
11 – Firemen

Islington

B1899
Station No. B67
B district

c1908
1 – steam fire engine
1 – horsed escape
1 – manual escape
1 – hose cart
1 – Station Officer
19 – Firemen
2 – Coachmen
2 – pairs of horses

c1965
Station No. C28
C division
Eastern Command
1 – pump escape
1 – pump
1 – Station Officer
1 – Sub Officer
1 – Leading Fireman
11 – Firemen

Redcross Street

B1900
Station No. B68
B district

c1908
2 – steam fire engines
1 – horsed escape
1 – long ladder
1 – manual escape
1 – hose cart
1 – Station Officer
24 – firemen
4 – Coachmen
3 – pairs of horses

West Hampstead

B1901
Station No. A20
A district
c1908
1 – steam fire engine
1 – horsed escape
1 – hose cart
1 – Station Officer
9 – firemen
2 – coachmen
2 – pairs of horses
c1965
Station No. G25
G division Northern
Command.
1 – pump escape
1 – turntable ladder
1 – Station Officer
1 – Sub Officer
1 – Leading Fireman
9 – Firemen
c2005
Station No. G51
Western Command.
1 – pump ladder
1 – pump
1 – Station Officer
1 – Sub Officer
1 – Leading Firefighter
10 - Firefighters

East Greenwich

B1901
Station No. D54
D district

c1908
1 – steam fire engine
1 – horsed escape
1 – manual escape
1 – hose cart
1 – manual engine
1 – Station Officer
9 – Firemen
2 – coachmen
2 – pairs of horses

c1965
Station No. E23
E division
Southern Command.
1 – pump escape
1 – pump
1 – turntable ladder
1 – Station Officer
1 – Sub Officer
2 – Leading Firemen
19 – firemen

Perry Vale

B1901
Station No. D55
D district

c1908
1 – steam fire engine
1 – horsed escape
1 – manual escape
1 – hose cart
1 – Station Officer
9 – Firemen
2 – coachmen
2- pairs of horses

c1965
Station No. E31
E division
Southern Command
1 – pump escape
1 – pump
1 – Station Officer
1 – Sub Officer
1 – Leading Fireman
11 - Firemen

Homerton

B1901
Station No. C23
C district

c1908
1 – steam fire engine
1 – horsed escape
1 – long ladder
1 – manual escape
1 – hose cart
1 – Station Officer
14 – Firemen
2 – coachmen
2 – pairs of horses

c1965
Station No. F28
F division
Eastern Command
1 – pump escape
1 – pump
1 – Station Officer
1 – Sub Officer
1 – leading Fireman
11 – Firemen

Euston

B1901
Station No. B73
B district

c1908
1 – motor fire engine
1 – motor tender
1 – manual fire engine
1 – horsed escape
1 – long ladder
1 – hose cart
Divisional Officer
(North)
1 – District Officer
1 – Station officer
17 – Firemen
3 – Coachmen
3 – pairs of horses

c1965
Station No. A23
A division
Northern Command
1 – pump escape
1 – pump
1 – turntable ladder
1 – emergency tender
1 – Station Officer
1 – Sub Officer
3 – Leading Firemen
22 – Firemen

c2005
Station No. G46
Western Command
1 – pump ladder
1 – pump
1 – Fire Rescue Unit
1 – Station Officer
1 – Sub Officer
2 – Leading
Firefighters
16 – Firefighters

Shepherds Bush

B1901
Station No.A15
A district

c1908
1 – steam fire engine
1 – horsed escape
1 – manual escape
1 – hose cart
1 – Station Officer
9 – Firemen
2 – coachmen
2 – pairs of horses

Highbury

B1902
Station No. B70
B district

c1908
1 – steam fire engine
1 – horsed escape
1 – manual escape
1 – hose cart
1 – Station Officer
9 – firemen
2 – coachmen
2 – pairs of horses

Vauxhall

B1902

Station No. E94
E district

c1908
1 – steam fire engine
1 – horsed escape
1 – manual escape
1 – hose cart
1 – Station Officer
10 – Firemen
2 – Coachmen
2 – pairs of horses

Clapham

B1902
Station No. E80
E district

c1908
1 – steam fire engine
1 – horsed escape
1 – manual escape
1 – long ladder
1 – hose cart
1 – hose + coal van
1 – trap
1 – Superintendent
1 – District Officer
17 – Firemen
3 – Coachmen
3 – pairs of horses

Pageant's Wharf

B1903

c1908
Station No. D50
D district
1 – steam fire engine
1 – horsed escape
1 – manual escape
1 – hose cart
1 – Station Officer
6 – Firemen
1 – Coachman
1 – pair of horses

c1965
Station No. B25
B division
Southern Command
1 – pump escape
1 – pump
1 – Station Officer
1 – Sub Officer
1 – Leading Fireman
11 – Firemen

Mile End

1903
rebuilt on existing site
c1908
Station No. C31
C district

1 – horsed fire engine
1 – horsed escape
1 – manual escape
 1 – hose cart
1 – Station Officer
11 – Firemen
2 – Coachmen
2 – pairs of horses

Old Kent Road

B1903
Station No. E82
E district

c1908
1 – steam fire engine
1 – horsed escape
1 – manual escape
1 – hose cart
1 – Station Officer
12 – Firemen
2 – Coachmen
2 – pairs of horses

c1965
Station No. B26
B division
Southern Command
1 – pump escape
1 – pump
1 – Station Officer
1 – Sub Officer
1 – Leading Fireman
11 – Firemen

Streatham sub Station

c1901
station No. 56c

1 – horsed escape
3 – Firemen
1 – Coachman
1 – pair of horses

Streatham

B1903
Station No. E90
E district

c1908
1 – steam fire engine
1 – horsed escape
1 – manual escape
1 – hose cart
1 – Station Officer
9 – Firemen
2 – Coachmen
2 – pairs of horses

Streatham

after the war showing
building after bomb
damage.

c1965
station No. K25
K division
Southern Command

1 – pump escape
1 – pump
1 – Station Officer
1 – Sub Officer
1 – Leading Fireman
11 – Firemen

Deptford

B1904
Station No. D41
D district

c1908
1 – steam fire engine
1 – horsed escape
1 – manual escape
1 – hose cart
1 – Station Officer
11 - Firemen
3 – Coachmen
2 – pairs of horses

c1965
Station No. B27
B division
Southern Command
1 – pump escape
1 – pump
1 – foam tender
1 – Station Officer
1 – Sub Officer
2 – Leading Firemen
13 - Firemen

c2005
Station No. E36
Southern Command

1 – pump ladder
1 – Sub Officer
1 – Leading Firefighter
5 – Firefighters

Bayswater

B1904
Station No. A17
A district

c1908
1 – horsed escape
1 – manual escape
1 – hose cart
1 – oil wagon
1 – Station Officer
5 – Firemen
1 – Coachman
1 – pair of horses

Kilburn

B1904
Station No. A18
A district

c1908
1 – horse escape
1 – manual escape
1 – hose cart
1 – Station Officer
5 – Firemen
1 – Coachman
1 – pair of horses

Burdett Road

B1904
Station No. C22
C district
c1908
1 – horsed escape
1 – manual escape
1 – hose cart
1 – Station Officer
5 – Firemen
1 – coachman
1 – pair of horses

c1965
Station No. F24
F division
Eastern Command
1 – pump escape
1 – pump
1 – Station Officer
1 – Sub Officer
1 – Leading Fireman
11 – Firemen

Wapping

B1904
Station No. C21
C district

c1908
1 – motor fire engine
1 – manual engine
1 – manual escape
1 – hose cart
1 – Station Officer
8 - Firemen

Eltham

B1904
Station No. D56
D district

c1908
1 – horsed escape
1 – manual
1 – hose cart
1 – Station Officer
5 – Firemen
1 – Coachman
1 – pair of horses

c1965
Station No. E30
E division
Southern Command

1 – pump escape
1 – pump
1 – Station Officer
1 - Sub Officer
1 – Leading Fireman
11 - Firemen

c2005
Station No. E30
Southern Command
1 – pump ladder
1 – Sub Officer
1 – Leading Firefighter
5 – Firemen

Kensington

B1904
Station No. A8
A district

c1908
1 – steam fire engine
1 – horsed escape
1 – manual escape
1 – hose cart
1 – Station Officer
10 – Firemen
2 - Coachmen
2 – pairs of horses

c1965
Station No. A28
A division
Northern Command

1 – pump escape
1 – pump
1 – turntable ladder
1 – Station Officer
1 – Sub Officer
2 – Leading Firemen
14 – firemen

c2005
Station No. G33
Western Command

1 – pump ladder
1 – pump
1 – Station Officer
1 – Sub Officer
1 – Leading Firefighter
10 – Firefighters

Isle of Dogs
(now Millwall)

B1904
station No. C35
C district

c1908
1 – steam fire engine
1 – horsed escape
1 – manual escape
1 – hose cart
1 – Station Officer
10 - Firemen
2 – Coachmen
2 – pairs of horses

c1965
Station No. F23
F division
Eastern Command

1 – pump escape
1 – pump
1 – Station Officer
1 – Sub Officer
1 – Leading Fireman
11 - Firemen

c2005
Station No. F23
Eastern Command
1 – pump ladder
1 – Sub Officer
1 – Leading Firefighter
5 – Firefighters

Westminster

B1905
station No. A3
A district

c1908
1 – steam fire engine
1 – horsed escape
1 – turntable long
ladder
1 – manual escape
1 – hose cart
1 – Station Officer
13 – Firemen
3 – Coachmen
3 – pairs of horses

c1965
Station No. A25
A division
Northern Command
1 – pump escape
1 – pump
1 – turntable ladder
1 – Station Officer
1 – Sub Officer
2 – Leading Firemen
14 - Firemen

c2005
Station No. G43
Western Command.
1 – pump ladder
1 – pump
1 – Station Officer
1 – Sub Officer
1 – Leading Firefighter
10 – Firefighters

Herne Hill

B1905
Station No. E93
E district

c1908
1 – horsed escape
1 – hose cart
1 – Station Officer
5 – Firemen
1 – coachman
1 – pair of horses

Northcote Road

B1905
Station No. E92
E district

c1908
1 – steam fire engine
1 – horsed escape
1 – long ladder
1 – manual escape
1 – hose cart
1 – Station Officer
12 – Firemen
2 – Coachmen
2 – pairs of horses

Lee Green

B1905	c1908	c1965	c2005
station No. D52	1 – motor fire engine	Station No. E29	Station No. E29
D district	1 – motor escape	E division	Southern Command
	1 – first aid motor appliance	Southern Command	1 – pump ladder
	1 – hose cart	1 – pump escape	1 – Sub Officer
	1 – Station Officer	1 - pump	1 – Leading Firefighter
	11 Firemen	1 – Station Officer	5 – Firefighters
		1 – Sub Officer	
		1 – Leading Fireman	
		11 – Firemen	

Brixton

B 1906
as two bay station
Station No. E85
E district
C1908
1 – steam fire engine
1 – horsed escape
1 – manual escape
2 – Hose carts
1 – Station Officer
11 – Firemen
2 – Coachmen
2 - pair of horses

c1965
Station No. B30
B division
Southern Command
now three bays.
1 – pump escape
1 – pump
1 – Turntable ladder
1 – Station Officer
1 – Sub Officer
2 – Leading Firemen
14 – Firemen

c2005
Station No. E46
Southern Command
1 – pump ladder
1 – pump
1 – Station Officer
1 – Sub Officer
1 – Leading Firefighter
10 – Firefighters

Cannon Street

B 1906

c1908
Station No. F63
F district.
1 – motor fire engine
1 – horsed fire engine
1 – horsed escape
1 – manual escape
1 - turntable long
ladder
1 – Station Officer
22 – Firemen
4 – Coachmen
3 - pair of horses

c1965
Station No. C25
C division
Eastern Command
1 – pump ladder
1 – pump
1 – turntable ladder
1 – Station Officer
1 – Sub Officer
2 – Leading Firemen
14 – Firemen

Plumstead

B1906

c1908
Station No. D57
D district
1 – horsed escape
1 – manual escape
1 – hose cart
1 – Station Officer
6 – Firemen
1 – Coachman
1 - pair of horses

c1965
Station No. E25
E division
Southern Command
1 – pump escape
1 – pump
1 – Station Officer
1 – Sub Officer
1 – Leading Fireman
11 – Firemen

c2005
Station No. E25
Southern Command
1 – pump ladder
1 – pump
1 – Station Officer
1 – Sub Officer
1 – Leading Firefighter
10 – Firefighters

Hornsey Rise

B 1906
Station No. B77
B district

c1908
1 – horsed escape
1 – manual escape
1 – hose cart
1 – Station Officer
5 – Firemen
1 – Coachman
1 - pair of horses

Knightsbridge

B 1907
Station No. A5
A district

c1908
1 – steam fire engine
1 – horsed escape
1 – horsed long ladder
1 – manual escape
1 – hose cart
1 – Station Officer
13 – Firemen
5 – Coachmen
3 – pairs of horses

c1965
Station No. A26
A division
Northern Command
1 – pump escape
1 – pump
1 – Station Officer
1 – Sub Officer
1 – Leading Fireman
11 – Firemen

c2005
Station No. G44
Western Command.
1 – pump ladder
1 – pump
1 – Station Officer
1 – Sub Officer
1 - Leading Firefighter
10 – Firefighters

Tooting

B1907
Station No. E86
E district

c1908
1 – motor fire engine
1 – motor tender
1 – motor escape
1 – manual escape
1 – hose cart
1 – Station Officer
11 – Firemen

c1965
Station No. K24
K division
Southern Command
1 – pump escape
1 – pump
1 – Station Officer
1 – Sub Officer
1 – Leading Fireman
11 - Firemen

c2005
Station No. E50
Southern Command
1- pump ladder
1 - pump
1 – Station Officer
1 – Sub Officer
1 – Leading Firefighter
10 - Firefighters

Charlton

B1908
Station No. D58
D district

c1913
1 – motor fire engine
1 – motor escape
1 – motor escape
(spare)
1 – hose cart
1 – Station Officer
11 – Firemen

Holloway

B1908	c1908	c1965
Station No. B76	1 – steam fire engine	Station No. C30
B district	1 – horsed escape	C division
	1 – manual escape	Eastern Command
	1 – manual fire engine	1 – pump escape
	1 – hose cart	1 – pump
	1 – Station Officer	1 – Station Officer
	10 - Firemen	1 – Sub Officer
	2 – Coachmen	1 – Leading fireman
	2 - pair of horses	11 – Firemen

Caledonian Road

B1909
station No. B69
B district

c1913
1 – motor escape
1 – manual escape
1 – oil wagon
1 – hose cart
1 – Station Officer
6 – Firemen

Brunswick Road

B 1910
Station No. C24
C division

c1913
1 – motor escape
1 – manual escape
1 – hose cart
1 – station Officer
11 – Firemen

c1965
Station No. F22
F division
Eastern Command
1 – pump escape
1 – pump
1 – turntable ladder
1 – Station Officer
1 – Sub Officer
2 – Leading Firemen
14 - Firemen

Waterloo

B1910

Station No. F60
F district

c1913
1 – motor fire engine
1 – horsed fire engine
1 – horsed escape
1 – manual escape
1 – Station Officer
16 – Firemen
2 – Coachmen
2 - pair of horses

Foxley Road

B1910

Station No. E95
E district

c1913
1 – horsed escape
1 – manual escape
1 – hose cart
1 – Station Officer
5 – Firemen
1 – Coachman
1 - pair of horses

Southwark FS

Alan Gilfrin collection
Extended 1911
showing new four bay
station to the left with
the yard entrance
centre and joined to the
earlier station.

c1913
Chief station No. F1.
2 – motor fire engines
1 – motor escape
1 – hose cart
4 – motor tenders
1 – motor lorry
1 – horsed fire engine
1 – turntable long
ladder
1 – motor car
2 – hose & coal vans
4 – motor cars

Chief Officer
1 – Divisional Officer
(south)
1 – Assistant
Divisional Officer
Senior Superintendent
1 – District Officer
8 – Station Officer
47 - Firemen
17 - Coachmen
3 pairs of horses

in addition there are in
reserve and for
training:
1 – horsed escape
1 – manual engine
14 – manual escapes
1 – hose & ladder truck
4 - ladder vans
2 – store vans
9 – horsed fire engines
3 – long ladders

5 – hose carts
1 - trap
1 – oil wagon
2 – trollies

c1965
part of Southern
Command B division
Station No. B23
1 – pump escape
1 – pump
1 – Station Officer
1 – Sub Officer
1 – Leading Fireman
11 – Firemen

c2004
station No. E33
Southern Command
1 – pump ladder
1 – Sub Officer
1 – Leading Firefighter
5 – Firefighters

Bow

B1911
Station No. C32
C district

c1913
1 – motor fire engine
1 – motor escape
1 – hose cart
1 – motor escape
(spare)
1 – Station Officer
11 – Firemen

c1965
Station No. F27
F division
Eastern Command
1 – pump escape
1 – pump
1 – Station Officer
1 – Sub Officer
1 – Leading Fireman
11 - Firemen

Shooters Hill

B1912
Station No. D44
D district

c1913
1 – motor fire engine
1 – motor escape
1 – manual escape
1 – hose cart
1 – Station Officer
12 – Firemen

c1965
Station No. E26
E division
Southern Command
1 – pump escape
1 – pump
1 – Station Officer
1 – Sub Officer
1 – Leading Fireman
11 – Firemen

Hammersmith

B1914
Station No. A9
A district
c1914
1 – motor fire engine
1 – manual escape
1 – long ladder
1 – hose cart
1 – Station Officer
9 – Firemen

c1965
Station No. D23
D division
Northern Command
1 – pump escape
1 – pump
1 – Station Officer
1 – Sub Officer
1 – Leading Fireman
11 - Firemen

Hackney

B1914
Station No. C29
C district
c1914
1 – motor fire engine
1 – motor escape
1 – manual escape
1 – hose cart
1 – Station Officer
12 – Firemen

Belsize

B1915
Part of Northern
Command
G division
station No. G26
1 – pump escape
1 – pump
1 – Station Officer
1 – Sub Officer
1 – Leading Fireman
11 – Firemen

c2005
station No. G49
Western Command
1 – pump ladder
1 – Sub Officer
1 – Leading Firefighter
5 - Firefighters

West Norwood

B1916

c1965
Station No. B31
B division
Southern Command
1 – pump escape
1 – pump
1 – Station Officer
1 – Sub Officer
1 – Leading Fireman
11 – Firemen

c2005
Station No. E51
Southern Command
1 – pump ladder
1 – pump
1 – Station Officer
1– Sub Officer
1 – Leading Firefighter
10 – Firefighters

Soho

Eric Billingham Collection

B1888.
the name of The London Salvage Corps still visible at the top. Station taken over by the Brigade c1922.

The station after the war showing how most of the building was severely damaged by enemy bombing.

c1965
Station No. A24
A division
Northern Command
1 – pump escape
1 – pump
1 – turntable ladder
1 – Station Officer
1 – Sub Officer
2 – Leading Firemen
14 – Firemen

Peckham

B1925

c1965
Station No. B28
B division
Southern Command
1 – pump escape
1 – pump
1 – Station Officer
1 – Sub Officer
1 – Leading Fireman
11 – Firemen

Dockhead

B1928

c1965
Station No. B24
B division
Southern Command
1 – pump escape
1 – pump
1 – turntable ladder
1 – Station Officer
1 – Sub Officer
2 – Leading Firemen
14 – Firemen

c2005
Station No. E34
Southern Command
1 – pump ladder
1 – pump
1 – Station Officer
1 – Sub Officer
1 – Leading Firefighter
10 – Firefighters
*Note; this station was
used for the TV series
London's Burning.*

Whitechapel

B1931
c1965
Station No. C24
C division
Eastern Command
1 – pump escape
1 – pump
1 – turntable ladder
1 – Station Officer
1 – Sub Officer
2 – Leading Firemen
14 – Firemen

c2005
Station No. F33
Eastern Command
1 – pump ladder
1 –pump
1 – Station Officer
1 – Sub Officer
1 – Leading Firefighter
10 – Firefighters

Downham

B 1932, appliance bay
on the left &
accommodation huts
on the right.

c1965
station No. H22
H division
Southern Command
1 – pump escape
1 – Sub Officer
1 – Leading Fireman
6 - Firemen

c2005
Station No. E32
Southern Command
1 – pump ladder
1 – Sub Officer
1 – Leading Firefighter
5 – Firefighters

Lambeth

B1937 Brigade
Headquarters & Fire
Station
Station No. B22
B division
Southern Command

c1965
1 – pump escape
1 – pump
1 – turntable ladder
1- emergency tender
1 – canteen van
Fireboat
2 – Station Officer
2 – Sub Officers
4 – Leading Firemen
32 – firemen

c2005 Brigade
Headquarters station
No. E44 Southern
Command

1 – pump ladder
1 - pump
1 – operational Fbt
1 – support Fbt
1 – Station Officer
2 – Sub Officers
2 – Leading
Firefighters
10 – Firefighters

Brigade Command
Support station
No. O20
1 – command unit
1 – brigade control unit
3 – Sub Officers
9 – Leading
Firefighters

Lambeth River
Station (pontoon).

Shadwell

B 1937
c1965
Station No. F25
F division
Eastern Command
1 – pump escape
1 - pump
1 – Station Officer
1 – Sub Officer
1 – Leading Fireman
11 - Firemen

c2005
Station No. F25
Eastern Command
1 – pump ladder
1 – Sub Officer
1 – Leading Firefighter
5 – Firefighters

Battersea

B1938

c1965
Station No. K23
K division
Southern Command
1 – pump escape
1 – pump
1 – foam tender
1 – Station Officer
1 – Sub Officer
2 – Leading Firemen
13 – Firemen

c2005
Station No. E48
Southern Command
1 – pump ladder
1 – fire rescue unit
1 – SRU
1 – Station Officer
1 – Sub Officer
1 – Leading Firefighter
11 - Firefighters

Wandsworth

B1957
c1965
Station No. K22
K division
Southern Command
1 – pump escape
1 – pump
1 – turntable ladder
1 – Station Officer
1 – Sub Officer
2 – leading firemen
14 – firemen

c2005
Station No.E49
Southern Command
1 – pump ladder
1 - pump
1 – Station Officer
1 – Sub Officer
1 – Leading Firefighter
10 – Firefighters

Greenwich

B 1959
c1965
Station No. E22
E division
Southern Command
1 – pump escape
1 – pump
1 – emergency tender
1 – Station Officer
1 – Sub Officer
2 – Leading Firemen
19 – Firemen

c2005
Station No. E22
Southern Command
1 – pump ladder
1 – pump
1 – hydraulic platform
1 – Station Officer
1 – Sub Officer
2 – Leading Firefighters
11 – Firefighters

Clapham

B 1962
c1965
Station No. B21
B divisional HQ
Southern Command
1 – pump escape
1 – pump
1 – breakdown lorry
1 – Bacv
1 - lorry
2 – cars
1 – Station Officer
1 – Sub Officer
2 – Leading Fireman
18 - Firemen

c2005
station No. E47
Southern Command
1 – pump ladder
1 – pump
1 – turntable ladder
1 – Station Officer
1 – Sub Officer
2 – Leading Firefighters
11 – Firefighters

Shoreditch

B1964
c1965
Station No. C21
C divisional HQ
Eastern Command
1 – pump escape
2 – pump
1 – emergency tender
1 – Bacv
1 – lorry
2 – cars
1 – Station Officer
1 – Sub Officer
3 – Leading Firemen
29 – Firemen

c2005
station No. F24
Eastern Command
1 – pump ladder
1 – pump
1 – Station Officer
1 – Sub Officer
1 – Leading Firefighter
10 – Firefighters

Barbican

B1964

c1965
Station No. C26
C division
Eastern Command
1 – pump escape
2 – pumps
1 – Station Officer
1 – Sub Officer
2 – Leading Firemen
15 – Firemen

Chapter 4

London Fire Brigade
Greater London Council (GLC) 1965-1986

Map of London's stations, 1971

The London Government Act of 1963, passed by Royal Assent in July 1963, approved the formation of the Greater London Council, abolition of the London County Council and Middlesex County Council, and that the GLC and new London Boroughs take over from April 1st 1965.

The London Fire Brigade and the GLC took over the Middlesex, Croydon, East Ham & West Ham Fire Brigades, as well as stations from Hertfordshire, Essex, Kent, & Surrey Fire Brigades. The stations, appliances and equipment as well as personnel and other non-uniformed staff.

After the war and from 1948 when the Brigades took control of their stations and of those that also passed over to them from pre war Brigades now defunct, some commenced a station building programme.

Middlesex had 38 stations but needed to replace and resite many reducing the total to eventually 28.

The stations that were transferred over to London in 1965 being:-

Edmonton	Southgate	Enfield *	Ponders End	Coombes Croft
Tottenham *	Hornsey	Finchley	Harrow	Stanmore
Mill Hill	Hendon	Willesden	Kilburn	Park Royal
Wembley	Northolt	Hillingdon	Ruislip	Ealing
Acton	Chiswick	Heston	Twickenham	Feltham
Hayes	Southall *			

Potters Bar transferred to Hertfordshire Fire Brigade and Sunbury and Staines transferred to Surrey Fire Brigade.

(*) these stations opened after April 1965 by London to replace Ponders End and Coombes Croft stations.

Croydon Fire Brigade transferred over to London in 1965:-

Croydon	Woodside	Thornton Heath	Addington

East Ham Fire Brigade transferred its only station at East Ham.

West Ham Fire Brigade transferred over to London in 1965:-

Stratford	Plaistow	Silvertown

Kent Fire Brigade transferred over to London in 1965:-

Bromley	Beckenham	Biggin Hill	Bexley
Sidcup	West Wickham	Orpington	Erith

Essex Fire Brigade transferred over to London in 1965:-

Ilford	Romford	Hornchurch	Dagenham
Barking	Leytonstone	Leyton	Walthamstow
Chingford	Woodford	Hainault	Wennington

Hertfordshire Fire Brigade(formerly the Hertfordshire Fire & Ambulance service),
Transferred over to London in 1965: -
East Barnet

Surrey Fire Brigade transferred over to London in 1965: -

Richmond	Kingston	Wimbledon	Mitcham	Malden
Surbiton	Wallington	Sutton	Purley	Sanderstead

The General Purposes Committee of the GLC and the full Council confirmed the appointment of Mr. Leete as the Chief Officer of the London Fire brigade, with Mr. Mummery as Deputy Chief Officer, formerly the Chief Officer of Middlesex Fire Brigade.

The organisation of the brigade was that it should be divided into three commands with eleven divisions, Northern Command with HQ at Wembley, with four divisions Eastern Command with HQ at Stratford, with three divisions and Southern Command with HQ at Croydon, with four divisions including the River Thames.

Mr. TW. Syrett Assistant Chief Officer (formerly DCO Middlesex FB), Northern Command Commander, in charge of former Middlesex FB stations, part of Hertfordshire and most of the former 'A' division of the old LFB. Divisional HQ's 'A' division A21 Manchester Square, 'D' division D21 Ealing, 'G' division G21 Harrow and 'J' division J21 Edmonton.

Mr. BE. Cutting Assistant Chief Officer (formerly Chief Officer West Ham FB), Eastern Command Commander, in charge of former West & East Ham FB stations, part of Essex and those of the former 'B' division of the old LFB. Divisional HQ's 'C' division C21 Shoreditch, 'F' division F21 Stratford and 'L' division L21 East Ham.

Mr RR.Lloyd Assistant Chief Officer (formerly Chief Officer Croydon FB), Southern Command Commander, in charge of the former Croydon FB stations, part of Kent & Surrey and those of the former 'C' & 'D' divisions of the old LFB. Divisional HQ's 'B' division B21 Clapham, 'E' Division E21 Lewisham, * 'H' division H21 Bromley and 'K' division K21 Wimbledon.

Stations and Divisions of the Western Command.

A21 Manchester Square	D21 Ealing
A22 Camden Town	D22 Acton
A23 Euston	D23 Hammersmith
A24 Soho	D24 Fulham
A25 Westminster	D25 Chiswick
A26 Knightsbridge	D26 Twickenham
A27 Chelsea	D27 Heston
A28 Kensington	D28 Feltham
A29 N.Kensington	D29 Southall
A30 Edgware Road	D30 Hayes
	D31 Hillingdon
G21 Harrow	J21 Edmonton
G22 Stanmore	J22 Chingford
G23 Mill Hill	J23 Woodford
G24 Hendon	J24 Walthamstow
G25 W.Hampstead	J25 Tottenham
G26 Belsize	J26 Hornsey
G27 Kilburn	J27 Finchley
G28 Willesden	J28 Southgate
G29 Park Royal	J29 Barnet
G30 Wembley	J30 Enfield
G31 Northolt	J31 Coombes Croft
G32 Ruislip	J32 Ponders End

Stations and Divisions of the Eastern Command.

C21 Shoreditch	F21 Stratford	L21 East Ham
C22 Kingsland	F22 Brunswick Road	L22 Ilford
C23 Stoke Newington	F23 Millwall	L23 Hainault
C24 Whitechapel	F24 Burdett Road	L24 Romford
C25 Cannon Street	F25 Shadwell	L25 Dagenham
C26 Barbican	F26 Bethnal Green	L26 Hornchurch
C27 Clerkenwell	F27 Bow	L27 Barking
C28 Islington	F28 Homerton	L28 Wennington
C29 Kentish Town	F29 Leyton	L29 Silvertown
C30 Holloway	F30 Leytonstone	L30 Plaistow

Stations and Divisions of the Southern Command.

B21 Clapham	E21 Lewisham *
B22 Lambeth	E22 Greenwich
B23 Southwark	E23 East Greenwich

B24 Dockhead	E24 Woolwich
B25 Pageant's Wharf	E25 Plumstead
B26 Old Kent Road	E26 Shooters Hill
B27 Deptford	E27 Erith
B28 Peckham	E28 Bexley
B29 New Cross**	E29 Lee Green
B30 Brixton	E30 Eltham
B31 West Norwood	E31 Perry Vale
H21 Bromley	K21 Wimbledon
H22 Downham	K22 Wandsworth
H23 Sidcup	K23 Battersea
H24 Orpington	K24 Tooting
H25 Biggin Hill	K25 Streatham
H26 Addington	K26 Mitcham
H27 West Wickham	K27 Wallington
H28 Woodside	K28 Sutton
H29 Purley	K29 Surbiton
H30 Sanderstead	K30 Malden
H31 Croydon	K31 Kingston
H32 Thornton Heath	K32 Richmond
H33 Beckenham	

(Reference above * & ** see below).

The attendance of appliances laid down by the Home Office were that three appliances should form the attendance for the inner London area formerly the LCC area and all special risk and 'A' risks in outer London while a two appliance attendance for category 'B' risks and outer London.

124 Fire Stations were under the control of the GLC, Clerkenwell being the oldest, built in 1870 (still in use in 2005), and the newest built at Barbican (though to eventually close due to government financial cuts), and Chiswick and both opened just before April 1965. Three more stations due to open in 1965 were Southall, Enfield and Tottenham this enabled five old stations to close. Since the end of the Second World War the LCC had planned to build 26 new stations, a programme that the GLC would continue. Plans for new stations at Paddington (divisional), Lewisham (divisional) and Knightsbridge, two extensions to Brigade Headquarters and new control room, and an extension to training at Southwark and Finchley, plus a residential school for junior firemen and two hostels for single men and married men looking for accommodation in London.

From 1967 the new station at Lewisham * will be opened as the 'E' divisional Headquarters, New Cross ** being the former HQ and now formed part of the 'B' division.

Plans for a new station at Bethnal Green, and new Divisional HQ at Poplar, (the divisional staff at present located at Stratford Fire Station), East India Dock Road which will replace stations at Burdett road and Brunswick Road. Camden Town and West Wickham stations closed.

1968, Pageants Wharf closed.

1969 saw new stations opened at Old Kent Road which replaced former station, Silvertown replaced station on existing site, Bexley replaced former station at Bexleyheath, Bethnal Green replaced former station and Paddington which replaced Edgware Road and Kilburn stations.

1970 Poplar station opened and replaced Brunswick Road.

1971 Norbury opened and replaced both Streatham and Thornton Heath Fire stations.

The firefighters not transferred to Norbury were deployed to Biggin Hill fire station where since the change over from Kent brigade to London had remained day manning but could now under the present establishment now change to the three watch system operated throughout the brigade.

1972 Homerton rebuilt on existing site, Kentish Town built on an adjacent site and Forest Hill built to replace Perry Vale station.

April the Brigade abolished the three command structure set up in 1965 to oversee the merger of the Brigades or part of those that had now become part of the new GLC/LFB. The eleven commanders now having direct control but as necessary within direct liaison with brigade HQ. An Operations Branch now established at brigade HQ to help obtain and to give information about risks to incident commanders and to inform and mobilize senior officers. The staff also crew the Brigade control unit based at HQ while the control units based at the three commands have now been withdrawn.

The brigade have also set up 'A Technical and Development Branch' for the technical research and operational development of the brigade. The 'H' divisional HQ at present based at the Bromley fire station will soon move to the Croydon fire station.

During the year the Brigade set up the first mobile Fire Investigation Team, the aim is to assist the investigation into the cause of fires and those of doubtful origin.

1974 Bow station rebuilt on existing site, Stoke Newington rebuilt.

1975 Holloway rebuilt, Kingsland Road rebuilt on existing site.

1976 Dowgate built to replace Cannon Street.

1978 New Malden built to replace Malden.

1983 Soho rebuilt on adjacent site opened in March at a cost of £2. 5 million, built as part of a commercial development. Builders now occupied the site for the new Beckenham fire station which is expected to cost £1 million.

1984. The site for a new station for L22 Ilford at Clarks Road, was handed over to the contractor, it is hoped to be completed in early 1986.

The Insurance Companies in 1984 decided to disband the Salvage Corps of London, Liverpool and Glasgow. London now had to take over salvage work at incidents as laid down by the Government act, taking on 5 new salvage tenders and the former HQ at Aldersgate Street City, since demolished.

1985 North Kensington rebuilt on adjacent site, Beckenham replaced. East Greenwich, new station built further along the road with two bays and large area for appliance to rear of these bays also the command foam reserve held here. One pumping appliance removed from here when the station at Heathrow became operational.

Government decided to abolish the Greater London Council and set up an Authority around the 32 Borough Councils and the City Corporation, a new authority namely "The London Fire & Civil Defence Authority" known as LFCDA, would now run the fire brigade and take over most of the non - uniform staff some previously employed at the County hall, the extra staff being placed at the new Command HQ's within the brigade. This new Authority would start from April 1986.

Malden

B 1890
Formerly Malden &
Coombe Local
Authority FB,
Part of Surrey FB
1948.

c1965
Station No. K30
K division
Southern Command
1 –pump escape
1 – hose layer
1 – Station Officer per
station
1 – Sub Officer
2 – Leading Firemen
8 – Firemen

Woodford

B 1900
formerly Woodford &
Wanstead Local
Authority FB. Part of
Essex FB 1948.

c1965
Station No. J23
J division
Northern Command

1 - pump escape
1 –Pump
1 – Station Officer
1 – Sub Officer
1 – Leading fireman
11 – firemen

Beckenham

B1904
Formerly Local
Authority FB
Formed part of the
Kent FB c1948
c1965
Station No. H33
H division
Southern Command

1 - pump ladder
1 – pump
1 – Station Officer per
station
1 – Sub officer
2 – Leading Firemen
11 – Firemen

Wimbledon

B 1904
Formerly Local
Authority FB
Part of the Surrey FB
1948
c1965
Station No. K21
K divisional HQ
Southern Command

1 – pump escape
1 – pump
1 – turntable ladder
1 – Bacv
1 – lorry
2 – cars
1 – Station officer per
station
1 – Sub Officer
1 – Station Officer
3 – Leading Firemen
19 – Firemen

Barnet

B 1905
Formerly Local
Authority FB.
Formed part of the
Hertfordshire FB 1948.

c1965
Station No. J29
J division
Northern Command
1 – water tender
1 – Station Officer per
station
1 – Sub Officer
1 – Leading Fireman
6 – Firemen

Ilford

B1905
Formerly Local
Authority FB
Part of Essex FB 1948.

c1965
Station No. L22
L division
Eastern Command

1 – pump escape
1 – pump
1 – Station Officer
1 – Sub Officer
1 – Leading Fireman
11 – Firemen

Sidcup

B1908
Formerly part of
Chislehurst & Sidcup
Local Authority FB.
Part of Kent FB c1948.

c1965
Station No. H23
H division
Southern Command
1 – water tender ladder
1 – pump
1 – Station Officer per
Station
1 – Sub Officer
2 – Leading Firemen
11 – Firemen

c2005
station No. E40
Southern Command
1 – pump ladder
1 – Sub Officer
1 – Leading Firefighter
5 – firefighters

Bromley

B1908
Formerly Local
Authority FB.
Part of Kent FB c1948.
c1965
Station No. H21
H divisional HQ
Southern Command
1 – pump ladder
1 – pump
1 – turntable ladder
1 – Bacv
1 – lorry
2 – cars
1 – Station Officer per
Station
1 – Sub Officer
3 – Leading Firemen
19 – Firemen
c2005 station No.E39
Southern Command
1 – pump ladder
1 – Station Officer
1 – pump
1 – Sub Officer
1 – Leading Firefighter
10 – Firefighters

Leytonstone

Formerly Local
Authority FB.
Part of Essex FB c1948.

c1965
Station No. F30
F division
Eastern Command

1 – pump escape
1 – pump
1 – Station Officer
1 – Sub Officer
1 – Leading Fireman
11 – Firemen

Silvertown photo

B1914
Formerly part of West
Ham FB.
c1965
Station No. L29
L division Eastern
Command

1 – pump escape
1 – pump
1 – Station Officer
1 – Sub Officer
1 – Leading Fireman
11 – Firemen

Thornton Heath

Part of Croydon FB.
c1965
Station No. H32
H division
Southern Command

1 – pump escape
1 – salvage tender
1 – Station Officer
1 – Sub Officer
1 – Leading Fireman
8 – Firemen

Leyton

B 1917
Part of Essex FB c1948.

c1965
Station No. F29
F division
Eastern Command

1 – pump escape
1 – Sub Officer
1 – Leading Fireman
6 - Firemen

Hendon

B1918
Formerly Local
Authority FB
Part of Middlesex FB
1948.

c1965
Station No. G24
G division
Northern Command

1 – pump escape
1 – pump
1 – turntable ladder
1 – hose layer
1 – Station Officer
1 – Sub Officer
3 – Leading Firemen
14 – Firemen

c2005 Station No. G52
Western Command.
1 – pump ladder
1 – Sub Officer
1 – Leading Firefighter
10 – Firefighters

Walthamstow

B1923
Formerly Local
Authority FB
Part of Essex FB c1948.

c1965
Station No. J24
J division
Northern Command
1 – pump escape
1 – pump
1 – Station Officer
1 – Sub Officer
1 – Leading Fireman
11 – Firemen

c2005
Station No. F36
Eastern Command.

1 – pump ladder
1 – Sub Officer
1 – Leading Firefighter
10 – Firefighters

Mitcham

B1928
Formerly Local
Authority FB
Part of Surrey FB
c1948.

c1965
Station No. K26
K division
Southern Command
1 – pump escape
1 – pump
1 – Station Officer per
station
1 – Sub Officer
2 – Leading Firemen
11 – Firemen

c2005
Station No. E53
Southern Command
1 – pump ladder
1 – Sub Officer
1 – Leading Firefighter
5 – Firefighters

Mill Hill

B1929
Part of Hendon Local
Authority FB.
Part of Middlesex FB
c1948.

c1965
Station No. G23
G division
Northern Command
1 – pump escape
1 – pump
1 – Station Officer
1 – Sub Officer
1 – Leading Fireman
11 – Firemen

c2005
Station No.G55
Western Command.

1 – pump ladder
1 – Sub Officer
1 – Leading Firefighter
5 – Firefighters

Purley

B1929
Part of Coulsdon &
Purley
Local Authority FB.
Part of Surrey FB
c1948.
c1965
Station No. H29
H division
Southern Command
1 – water tender
1 – Station Officer per
station
1 – Sub Officer
1 – Leading Fireman
6 – Firemen

c2005
Station No. E60
Southern Command.
1 – pump ladder
1 – Sub Officer
1 – Leading Firefighter
5 – Firefighters

Bexley

Formerly Local
Authority FB.
Part of Kent FB c1948.
c1965
Station No. E28
E division
Southern Command
1 – pump
1 – water tender ladder
1 – Station Officer per
station
1 – Sub Officer
2 – Leading Firemen
11 – Firemen

Plaistow

B1931
Formerly part of West
Ham FB.
c1965
Station No. L30
L division
Eastern Command

1 – pump escape
1 – pump
1 – turntable ladder
1 – Station Officer
1 – Sub Officer
2 – Leading Firemen
14 - firemen

c2005
Station No. F45
Eastern Command.
1 – pump ladder
1 – pump
1 – Station Officer
1 – Sub Officer
1 – Leading Firefighter
11 – Firefighters

Surbiton

B 1931
Formerly Local
Authority FB, Part of
Surrey FB 1948.
c1965
Station No. K29
K division
Southern Command
1 – pump escape
1 – Station Officer per
station
1 – Sub Officer
1 – Leading Fireman
6 - Firemen

c2005
Station No. E56
Southern Command.
1 – pump ladder
1 – Sub Officer
1 – Leading Firefighter
5 - Firefighters

Woodside

B1932
Part of Croydon Local
Authority FB.
c1965
Station No. H28
H division
Southern Command
1 – pump escape
1 – pump
1 – Station Officer
1 – Sub Officer
1 – Leading Fireman
11 – Firemen

c2005
Station No. E62
Southern Command.
1 – pump ladder
1 – Sub Officer
1 – Leading Firefighter
10 – Firefighters

Ealing

B1933
Formerly Local
Authority FB
Part of Middlesex FB
c1948.
c1965
Station No. D21
D divisional HQ
Northern Command
1 – pump escape
1 – pump
1 – Bacv
1 – lorry
2 – cars
1 – Station Officer
1 – Sub Officer
1 – Leading Fireman
16 – Firemen
c2005
Station No. G25
Western Command.
1 – pump ladder
1 – pump
1 – Station Officer
1 – Sub Officer
1 – Leading Firefighter
10 – Firefighters

Willesden

B1934
formerly local
authority FB
Part of Middlesex FB
c1948.
c1965
Station No. G28
G division
Northern Command
1 – pump escape
1 – pump
1 – Station Officer
1 – Sub Officer
1 – Leading Fireman
10 – Firemen

c2005
Station No. G28
Western Command
1 – pump ladder
1 - pump
1 – Station Officer
1 – Sub Officer
1 – Leading Firefighter
10 – Firefighters

Barking

B1935
formerly local
authority FB part of
Essex FB
c1948
c1965
Station No. L27
L division
Eastern Command
1 – pump escape
1 – pump
1 – salvage tender
1 – hose layer
1 – Station Officer
1 – Sub Officer
3 – Leading Firemen
14 – Firemen
c2005 Station No. F43
Eastern Command
1 – pump ladder
1 – pump
2 – Pm's
various pod's
1 – Station Officer
1 – Sub Officer
1 – Leading Firefighter
14 - Firefighters

Finchley

B1935
formerly local
authority FB Part of
Middlesex FB c1948.

c1965
Station No. J27
J division
Northern Command
1 – pump escape
1 – emergency tender
1 – Station Officer
1 – Sub Officer
1 – Leading Fireman
12 – Firemen

c2005
Station No. G53
Western Command
1 – pump ladder
1 – Sub Officer
1 – Leading Firefighter
5 – Firefighters

Heston

Authors collection
B1936
formerly Heston &
Isleworth local
authority FB Part of
Middlesex FB c1948.

c1965
Station No. D27
D division
Northern Command
1 – pump escape
1 – pump
1 – turntable ladder
1 – emergency tender
1 – foam tender
1 – Station Officer
1 – Sub Officer
4 – Leading Firemen
21 – Firemen

c2005
Station No. G38
Western Command
1 – pump ladder
1 – Fire rescue Unit
1 – Station Officer
1 – Sub Officer
1 – Leading Firefighter
11 - Firefighters

Sanderstead

B1936 part of Surrey
FB

c1965
Station No. H30
H division
Southern Command
1 – water tender
1 Station Officer per
station
1 – Sub Officer
1 – Leading Fireman
6 – Firemen

Harrow

B1937 formerly local
authority FB part of
Middlesex FB c1948.

c1965
Station No. G21
G divisional HQ
Northern Command
1 – pump escape
1 – pump
1 – hose layer
1 – Bacv
1 – lorry
2 – cars
1 – Station Officer
1 – Sub Officer
2 – Leading Firemen
18 – Firemen

c2005
Station No. G21
Western Command
1 – pump ladder
1 – Sub Officer
1 – Leading Firefighter
5 - Firefighters

Acton

B1938
formerly local
authority FB
Part of Middlesex FB
c1948.
c1965
Station No. D22
D division
Northern Command
1 – pump escape
1 – pump
1 – turntable ladder
1 – Station Officer
1 – Sub Officer
2 – Leading Firemen
14 – Firemen

c2005
Station No. G26
Western Command
1 – pump ladder
1 – pump
1 – Station Officer
1 – Sub Officer
1 – Leading Firefighter
10 – Firefighters

Dagenham

B1938
formerly local
authority FB
Part of Essex FB c1948.
c1965
Station No. L25
L division
Eastern Command
1 – pump escape
1 – pump
1 – turntable ladder
1 – Station Officer
1 – Sub Officer
2 – Leading Firemen
14 – firemen

c2005
Station No. F41
Eastern Command
1 – pump ladder
1 – pump
1 – hydraulic platform
1 – Station Officer
1 – Sub Officer
2 – Leading Firefighters
11 - Firefighters

Wallington

B 1938
Formerly Beddington
& Wallington Local
Authority FB.
Part of Surrey FB
1948.

c1965
Station No. K27
K division
Southern Command
1 – pump escape
1 – Station Officer per
station
1 – Sub Officer
1 – Leading Fireman
6 - Firemen

c2005
Station No. E59
Southern Command
1 – pump ladder
1 – Sub Officer
1 – Leading Firefighter
5 - Firefighters

West Wickham

B1939
Part of Kent FB C1948

c1965
Station No. H27
H division
Southern Command
1 – water tender
1 – station Officer per
station
1 – Sub Officer
1 – Leading Fireman
6 - firemen

Wembley

B 1939
Formerly Local
Authority FB
Part of Middlesex FB
1948.

c1965
Station No. G30
G division
Northern Command
HQ
1 – pump escape
1 – pump
1 – turntable ladder
1 – Station Officer
1 – Sub Officer
2 – Leading Firemen
14 Firemen

c2005
Station No. G30
Western Command,
Command HQ Station
No. G20
G30
1 – pump ladder
1 – pump
1 – aerial ladder
platform
1 – Station Officer
1 – Sub Officer
2 – Leading
Firefighters
11 – Firefighters
G20
1 – CU
1 – Staff Sub Officer
6 – Leading
Firefighters

Biggin Hill

B1940
Formerly part of
Orpington local
authority FB.
Part of Kent FB. c1948.

c1965
Station No. H25
H division
Southern Command
1 – water tender ladder
1 – Station Officer per
station
1 – Sub Officer
1 – Leading Fireman
6 – Firemen

c2005
Station No. E42
Southern Command
1 – pump ladder
1 – Sub Officer
1 – Leading Firefighter
5 – Firefighters

Edmonton

B 1941.
Formerly Local
Authority FB
Part of Middlesex FB
1948 & divisional HQ
c 1965
Station No. J21
J divisional HQ
Northern Command
1 – pump escape
1 – pump
1 – foam tender
1 – Bacv
1 – lorry
2 – cars
1 – Station Officer
1 – Sub officer
2 – Leading firemen
18 Firemen

c 2005
Station No. F54
Eastern Command
1 – pump ladder
1 – pump
2 – prime movers
various pods
1 – Station Officer
1 – Sub Officer
1 – Leading Firefighter
14 – Firefighters

Hainault

B 1952
part of Essex FB C1948

c1965
Station No. L23
L division
Eastern Command
1 – pump escape
1 – pump
1 – Station Officer
1 – Leading Fireman
11 – Firemen

c2005
Station No. F37
Eastern Command
1 – pump ladder
1 – Sub Officer
1 – Leading Firefighter
5 – Firefighters

Chingford

AG collection
B 1957
Formerly local
authority FB
Part of Essex FB c1948

c1965
Station No. J22
J division
Northern Command
1 – pump escape
1 – pump
1 – Station Officer
1 – Sub Officer
1 – Leading Fireman
11 – Firemen

c2005
Station No. F34
Eastern Command
1 – pump ladder
1 – Sub Officer
1 – Leading Firefighter
5 – Firefighters

Orpington

AG collection
B1958
Formerly local
Authority FB
Part of Kent FB c1948

c1965
Station No. H24
H division
Southern Command
1 – water tender ladder
1 – Station Officer per station
1 – Sub Officer
1 – Leading Fireman
6 – Firemen

c2005
Station No. E41
Southern Command
1 – pump ladder
1 – Sub Officer
1 – Leading Firefighter
5 – Firefighters

Kingston

B1959 Formerly Local
Authority FB
Part of Surrey FB 1948

c1965
Station No. K31
K division
Southern Command
1 – pump escape
1 – water tender ladder
1 – turntable ladder
1 – Station Officer per station
1 – Sub Officer
3 – leading Firemen
14 - Firemen

c2005
Station No. E55
Southern Command
1 – pump ladder
1 - pump
1 – Station Officer
1 – Sub Officer
1 – Leading Firefighter
10 – Firefighters

Twickenham

AG collection
B 1959
Formerly Local
Authority FB
Part of Middlesex FB
1948.

c1965
Station No. D26
D division
Northern Command
1 – pump escape
1 – pump
1 – Station Officer
1 – Sub Officer
1 – Leading Fireman
11 Firemen

c2005
Station No. G41
Western Command
1 – pump ladder
1- IRU
1 – Sub Officer
1 – Leading Firefighter
5 – Firefighters

East Ham

B1959
Local authority FB

c1965
Station No. L21
L divisional HQ
Eastern Command
1 – pump escape
1 – pump
1 – emergency tender
1 – foam tender
1 - Bacv
1 – lorry
2 – cars
1 – Station Officer
1 – Sub Officer
3 – Leading Firemen
24 – Firemen
c2004
Station No. E55
Southern Command
1 – pump ladder
1 - pump
1 – Station Officer
1 – Sub Officer
1 – Leading Firefighter
10 – Firefighters

Park Royal Photo

Author's Collection

B 1960
part of Willesden Local
Authority FB part of
Middlesex FB 1948

c1965
Station No. G29
G division
Northern Command
1 – pump escape
1 – pump
1 – Station Officer
1 – Sub Officer
1 – Leading Fireman
11 - Firemen

c2005
Station No. G29
Western Command
1 – pump ladder
1 – IRU
1 – Sub Officer
1 – Leading Firefighter
7 – Firefighters

Feltham

Formerly local
authority FB
Part of Middlesex FB
c1948

c1965
Station No. D28
D division
Northern Command
1 – pump escape
1 – water tender
1 – Station Officer
1 – Sub Officer
1 – Leading Fireman
11 - Firemen

c2005
Station No. G39
Western Command
1 – pump ladder
1 – pump
1 – Station Officer
1 – Sub Officer
1 – Leading Firefighter
10 – Firefighters

Romford

B1960
part of Essex FB c1948

c1965
Station No. L24
L division
Eastern Command
1 – pump escape
1 – pump
1 – Station Officer
1 – Sub Officer
1 – Leading Fireman
11 – Firemen

c2005
part of Eastern
Command station No.
F38
1 – pump ladder
1 – pump
1 – Station Officer
1 – Sub Officer
1 – Leading Firefighter
10 – Firefighters

Stanmore

B1960 part of
Middlesex FB
c1965
Station No. G22
G division
Northern Command
1 – pump escape
1 – pump
1 – Station Officer
1 – Sub Officer
1 – Leading Fireman
11 – Firemen

c2005
Station No. G22
Western Command
1 – pump ladder
1 - IRU
1 – Sub Officer
1 – Leading Firefighter
5 – Firefighters

Addington

B1960 formerly part of
Croydon Fire Brigade
c1965
Station No. H26
H division
Southern Command
1 – pump escape
1 – Sub Officer
1 – Leading Fireman
6 – Firemen

c2005
Station No. E63
Southern Command
1 – pump ladder
1 – Sub Officer
1 – Leading Firefighter
5 - Firefighters

Croydon

B 1961 Formerly Local
Authority FB

c 1965
Station No. H31
H division Southern
Command HQ
1 – pump escape
1 – pump
1 – turntable ladder
1 – emergency tender
1 – Station Officer
1 – Sub Officer
3 – Leading Firemen
20 Firemen

c2005
Station No. E61
Southern Command
1 – pump ladder
1 - pump
1 - IRU
1 – Station Officer
1 – Sub Officer
1 – Leading Firefighter
10 – Firefighters

Erith

B1961 Formerly local
authority FB. Part of
Kent FB C1948.

c1965
Station No. E27
E division
Southern Command
1 – water tender ladder
1 – foam tender
1 – Station Officer per
station
1 – Sub Officer
2 – Leading Firemen
8 – Firemen

c2005
Station No. E27
Southern Command
1 – pump ladder
1 – pump
1 – Station Officer
1 – Sub Officer
1 – Leading Firefighter
10 – Firefighters

Hayes

B 1961 Formerly Hayes
& Harlington Local
Authority FB. Part of
Middlesex FB1948.
c1965
Station No. D30
D division
Northern Command
1 – pump escape
1 – pump
1 – turntable ladder
1 – hose layer
1 – Station Officer
1 – Sub Officer
3 - Leading Firemen
16 Firemen

c2005
Station No. G40
Western Command
1 – pump ladder
1 - pump
1- hydraulic platform
2 – prime movers
various pods
1 – Station Officer
1 – Sub Officer
2 – Leading Firefighter
15 – Firefighters

Ruislip

B 1961 Formerly
Ruislip & Northwood
Local Authority FB.
Part of Middlesex FB
1948.

c1965
Station No. G32
G division
Northern Command
1 – pump escape
1 – pump
1 – Station Officer
1 – Sub Officer
1 – Leading Fireman
11 – Firemen

c2005
Station No. G32
Western Command
1 – pump ladder
1 – Sub Officer
1 – Leading Firefighter
5 – Firefighters

Southgate

JBN collection
B1961 formerly Local
Authority FB
Part of Middlesex FB
c1948

c 1965
Station No. J28
J division
Northern Command
1 – pump escape
1 – pump
1 – salvage tender
1 – Station Officer
1 – Sub Officer
2 – Leading Firemen
13 – Firemen

c2005
Station No. F56
Eastern Command
1 – pump ladder
1 – Sub Officer
1 – Leading Firefighter
5 - Firefighters

Hornsey

B1962
Formerly local
authority FB
Part of Middlesex FB
c1948

c1965
Station No. J26
J division
Northern Command
1 – pump escape
1 – pump
1 – Station Officer
1 – Sub Officer
1 – Leading fireman
11 – Firemen

c2005
Eastern Command
station No. A32
1 – pump ladder
1 – pump
1 – Station Officer
1 – Sub Officer
1 – Leading Firefighter
10 – Firefighters

Northolt

B1962
AG collection
Part of Middlesex FB
c1965
Station No. G31
G division
Northern Command
1 – pump escape
1 – pump
1 – Station Officer
1 – Sub Officer
1 – Leading Fireman
11 - Firemen

c2005
Station No. G31
Western Command
1 – pump ladder
1 – Sub Officer
1 – Leading Firefighter
5 – Firefighters

Sutton

B1962 Formerly local
authority FB
part of Surrey FB
c1948

c1965
Station No. K28
K division
Southern Command
1 – pump escape
1 – pump
1 – Station Officer per
station
1 – Sub Officer
1 – Leading Fireman
11 – Firemen

c2005
Station No. E58
Southern Command
1 – pump ladder
2 – prime movers
various pods
1 – Sub Officer
1 – Leading Firefighter
9 – Firefighters

Wennington

B1962 part of Essex FB

c1965
Station No. L28
L division
Eastern Command
1 – pump escape
1 – Sub Officer
1 – Leading Fireman
6 – Firemen

c2005
Station No. F40
Eastern Command
1 – pump ladder
1 – IRU
1 – Sub Officer
1 – Leading Firefighter
5 - Firefighters

Hillingdon

B1963 part of
Middlesex FB

c1965
Station No. D31
D division
Northern Command
1 – pump escape
1 – pump
1 – Station Officer
1 – Sub Officer
1 – Leading Fireman
11 – Firemen

c2005
Station No. G23
Western Command
1 – pump ladder
1 – Sub Officer
1 – Leading Firefighter
5 – Firefighters

Richmond

B1963 formerly local
authority FB
Part of Surrey FB 1948

c1965
Station No. K32
K division
Southern Command
1 – pump escape
1 – pump
1 – Station Officer per
station
1 – Sub Officer
2 – Leading Firemen
11 – Firemen

c 2005
Station No. G42
Western Command
1 – pump ladder
1 – Sub Officer
1 – Leading Firefighter
5 - Firefighters

Chiswick

B1964
formerly Chiswick &
Brentford local
authority FB
Part of Middlesex
FB.c1948

c1965
Station No. D25
D division
Northern Command
1 – pump escape
1 – pump
1 – Station Officer
1 – Sub Officer
1 – Leading Fireman
11 – Firemen

c2005
Station No. G37
Western Command
1 – pump ladder
1 – Sub Officer
1 – Leading Firefighter
5 – Firefighters

Hornchurch

B1964 part of Essex FB

c1965
Station No. L26
L division
Eastern Command
1 – pump escape
1 – pump
1 – Station Officer
1 – Sub Officer
1 – Leading Fireman
11 – Firemen

c2005
Station No. F39
Eastern Command
1 – pump ladder
1 – Sub Officer
1 – Leading Firefighter
5 – Firefighters

Stratford

B1964 Part of West
Ham FB & Brigade
HQ.

c1965
Station No. F21
F divisional HQ,
Eastern Command HQ
1 – pump escape
1 – turntable ladder
1 – lorry
1 - pump
1 - Bacv
2 - cars
1– Station Officer
1 – Sub Officer
2 – leading Firemen
19 – Firemen

c2005
Station No. F21
Eastern Command,
Command HQ station
No. F20
F21
1 – pump ladder
1 – pump
1 – Station Officer
1 – Leading Firefighter
1 – Sub Officer
10 – Firefighters
F20
1 – CU
1 – Staff Sub Officer
6 – Leading
Firefighters

c2005
Brigade back-up
mobilising control.

Southall

B1965
Formerly local
authority FB
Part of Middlesex FB
c1948
c1965
Station No. D29
D division
Northern Command
1 – pump escape
1 – pump
1 – salvage tender
1 – Station Officer
1 – Sub Officer
2 – Leading Firemen
13 – Firemen

c2005
Station No. G24
Western
1 – pump ladder
1 – pump
1 – Station Officer
1 – Sub Officer
1 – Leading Firefighter
10- Firefighters

Chelsea

B1965

C1965
Station No. A27
A division
Northern Command
1 – pump escape
1 – pump
1 – hose layer
1 – Station Officer
1 – Sub Officer
2 – Leading Firemen
13 – Firemen

c2005
Station No. G34
Western Command
1 – pump ladder
1 – pump
1 – Station Officer
1 – Sub Officer
1 – Leading Firefighter
10 - Firefighters

Enfield

AG collection
Formerly local
authority FB
Part of Middlesex FB
c1948
c1965
Station No. J30
J division
Northern Command
1 – pump escape
1 – water tender
1 – hose layer
1 – Station Officer
1 – Sub Officer
2 – Leading Firemen
13 – Firemen

c2005
Station No. F55
Eastern Command
1 – pump ladder
1 – pump
1 – Station Officer
1 – Sub Officer
1 – Leading Firefighter
10 - Firefighters

Tottenham

B1966
Formerly local
authority FB
Part of Middlesex FB
c1948
c1965
Station No. J25
J division
Northern Command
1 – pump escape
1 – pump
1 – turntable ladder
1 – Station Officer
1 – Sub Officer
2 – Leading Firemen
14 – Firemen
c2005
Station No. F53
Eastern Command
1 – pump ladder
1 – pump
1 – ALP
1 – Station Officer
1 – Sub Officer
2 – Leading Firefighters
11 – Firefighters

Lewisham

B1967

c1967
Station No. E21
E divisional HQ
Southern Command
1 – pump escape
1 – pump
1 – hose layer
1 – Bacv
1 – lorry
2 – cars
1 – Station Officer
1 – Sub Officer
2 – Leading Firemen
18 - Firemen
Staff Sub Officer

c2005
Station No. E21
Southern Command,
Command HQ station
No. E20
E21
1 – pump ladder
1 – FRU
1 – Station Officer
1 – Sub Officer
1 – Leading Firefighter
11 – Firefighters
E20
1 – CU
1 – Staff Sub Officer
6 – Leading
Firefighters

Silvertown

B1968

c1968
Station No. L29
L division
Eastern Command
1 – pump escape
1 – pump
1 – Station Officer
1 – Sub Officer
1 – Leading Fireman
11 – Firemen

c2005
Station No. F46
Eastern Command
1 – pump ladder
1 – Sub Officer
1 – Leading Firefighter
5 – Firefighters

Bethnal Green

B1969

c1969
Station No. F26
F division
Eastern Command
1 – pump escape
1 – pump
1 – Station Officer
1 – Sub Officer
1 – Leading Fireman
11 – Firemen

c2005
Station No. F26
Eastern Command
1 – pump ladder
1 – pump
1 – Station Officer
1 – Sub Officer
1 – Leading Firefighter
10 – Firefighters

Bexley

B1969
Station No. E28
E division
Southern Command
1 – pump escape
1 – water tender ladder
1 – Station Officer
1 – Sub Officer
1 – Leading Fireman
11 – Firemen

c2005
Station No. E28
Southern Command
1 – pump ladder
1 – IRU
1 – Sub Officer
1 – Leading Firefighter
5 – Firefighters

Old Kent Road

B1969
Station No.B26
B division
Southern Command
1 – pump escape
1 – pump
1 – Station Officer
1 – Sub Officer
1 – Leading Fireman

c2005
Station No. E35
Southern Command
1 – pump ladder
1 – pump
1 – turntable ladder
1 – Station Officer
1 – Sub Officer
2 – Leading
Firefighters
11 – Firefighters

Paddington

B1969 replacing
Manchester square as
div HQ
c1969
Station No. A21
A divisional HQ
Northern Command
1 – pump escape
1 – pump
1 – turntable ladder
1 – Bacv
1 – lorry
2 – cars
1 – Station Officer
1 – Sub Officer
2 – Leading Firemen
19 – Firemen
staff Sub Officer
c2005
Station No. G48
Western Command
1 – pump ladder
1 – pump
1 – turntable ladder
1 - SRU
1 – Station Officer
1 – Sub Officer
2 – Leading
Firefighters
13 – Firefighters

Poplar

B1970
Station No. F22
F division
Eastern Command,
replacing Stratford as
the
F divisional HQ
station No. F22
c1970
1 – pump escape
1 – pump
1 – turntable ladder
1 – Station Officer
1 – Sub Officer
2 – Leading Firemen
14 – Firemen

c2005
Station No. F22
Eastern Command
1 – pump ladder
1 – pump
1 – Station Officer
1 – Sub Officer
1 – Leading Firefighter
10 – Firefighters

Norbury

c1971
station No. H32
H division
Southern Command
1 – pump escape
1 – Pump
1 – Station Officer
1 – Sub Officer
1 – Leading Fireman
10 – Firemen

c2005
Station No. E52
Southern Command
1 – pump ladder
1 – pump
1 – Station Officer
1 – Sub Officer
1 – Leading Firefighter
10 - Firefighters

Forest Hill

B1972

c1972
Station No. E31
E division
1 – pump escape
1 – pump
1 – Station Officer
1 – Sub Officer
1 – Leading Fireman
11 – Firemen

c2005
Station No. E31
Southern Command
1 – pump ladder
1 – pump
1 – ALP
1 – Station Officer
1 – Sub Officer
2 – Leading Firefighters
11 – Firefighters

Kentish Town

B1972

C1972
Station No. C29
C division
1 – pump escape
1 - pump
1 – Station Officer
1 – Sub Officer
1 – Leading Fireman
11 – Firemen

c2005
Station No. G50
Western Command
1 – pump ladder
1 – pump
1 – Station Officer
1 – Sub Officer
1 – Leading Firefighter
10 - Firefighters

Homerton

AG collection
B1972

c1972
Station No. F28
F division
1 – pump escape
1 – pump
1 – Station Officer
1 – Sub Officer
1 – Leading Fireman
10 – Firemen

c2005
Station no. F28
Eastern Command
1 – pump ladder
1 - pump
1 – Station Officer
1 – Sub Officer
1 – Leading Firefigher
10 – Firefighters

Bow

Author's collection
B1974

c1974
station No. F27
F division
1 – pump escape
1 – pump
1 – Station Officer
1 – Sub Officer
10 – firemen

c2005
Station No. F27
Eastern Command
1 – pump ladder
1 – pump
1 – Station Officer
1 – Sub Officer
1 – Leading Firefighter
10 - Firefighters

Stoke Newington

B1974

c1974
station No. C23
C division
1 – pump escape
1 – pump
1 – Station Officer
1 – Sub Officer
1 – Leading Fireman
10 – Firemen

c2005
Station No. F32
Eastern Command
1 – pump ladder
1 – pump
1 – Station Officer
1 – Sub Officer
1 – Leading Firefighter
10 – Firefighters

Holloway

B1975
Station No. C30
C division
c1975
1 – pump escape
1 – pump
1 – Station Officer
1 – Sub Officer
1 – Leading Fireman
10 – Firemen

c2005
Station No. F51
Eastern Command
1 – pump ladder
1 – pump
1 – Station Officer
1 – Sub Officer
1 – Leading Firefighter
10 – Firefighters

Kingsland

B1975

c1975
Station No. C22
C division
1 – pump escape
1 – pump
1 – Turntable ladder
1 – Station officer
1 – Sub Officer
2 – Leading Firemen
14 – Firemen

c2005
Station No. F31
Eastern Command
1 – pump ladder
1 – pump
1 – IRU
1 – Station Officer
1 – Sub Officer
1 – Leading Firefighter
11 – Firefighters

Dowgate

B1976

c1976
Station No. C25
C division
1 – pump escape
1 – pump
1 – Station Officer
1 – Sub Officer
1 – Leading Fireman
10 – Firemen

c2005
Station No. F48
Eastern Command
1 – pump ladder
1 – Sub Officer
1 – Leading Firefighter
5 – Firefighters

New Malden

AG collection
B1977

c1977
Station No. K30
K division
1 – pump escape
1 – hose layer
1 – Sub Officer
2 – Leading Firemen
7 – Firemen

c2005
Station No E57
Southern Command
1 – pump ladder
1 – Sub Officer
1 – Leading Firefighter
5 – Firefighters

Soho

B1983
c1983
Station No. A24
A division
1 – Pump ladder
1 – pump
1 – turntable ladder
1 – Station Officer
1 – Sub Officer
2 – Leading
Firefighters
14 – Firefighters

c2005
Station No. G45
Western Command
1 – pump ladder
1 – pump
1 – turntable ladder
1 – Station Officer
1 – Sub Officer
2 – Leading Firefighters
11 – Firefighters

Beckenham

B1985

c1985
Station No.H33
H division
1 – pump ladder
1 – pump
1 – Station Officer
1 – Sub Officer
1 – Leading Firefighter
10 – Firefighters

c2005
Station No. E43
Southern Command
1 – pump ladder
2 – Pm's
various pods
1 – Sub Officer
1 – Leading Firefighter
9 – Firefighters

East Greenwich

Author's collection
B1985

c1985
Station No. E23
E division
1 – pump ladder
1 – pump
1 – Station Officer
1 – Sub Officer
1 – Leading Firefighter
10 – Firefighters

c2005
Station No. E23
Southern Command
1 – pump ladder
1 – IRU
1 – Sub Officer
1 – Leading Firefighter
7 - Firefighters

North Kensington

B1985

c1985
station No. A29 North
West Area Command
1 – pump ladder
1 – pump
1 – Station Officer
1 – Sub Officer
1 – Leading Firefighter
10 – Firefighters

c2005
Station No. G27
Western Command
1 – pump ladder
1 – pump
1 – Station Officer
1 – Sub Officer
1 – Leading Firefighter
10 – Firefighters

Chapter 5

London Fire & Civil Defence Authority (LFCDA) 1986-2000

Map of the London Fire Brigade c 1992

1986. The new Command structure of the brigade commenced with the setting up of a five Command structure with Area Command HQ's at Wembley, Paddington, Stratford, Croydon and Lewisham.

The LFCDA approved £1 million for improvements to the Area headquarters at Lewisham, Stratford and Croydon. Stratford to have a two-storey building for the Headquarters staff and improvements both at the Lewisham and Croydon stations.

Approval for the replacement of Wimbledon fire station, which will be built at a cost of £1.5 million. The developers Speyhawk will pay for the building that will be located at Kingston Road and then re-develop the existing site within the new town plans.

1987. The station at Ilford officially opened.

1988. Wimbledon replaced on new site.

1989. LFCDA invite tenders for the building of a new fire station to replace the existing Islington station with estimate of £3 million.

1990. Brigade control 'CMC', (Command & Mobilising Centre), opened and replaced the Brigade controls at Croydon, Wembley and Stratford and the old Operations room based at HQ.

1991. Peckham rebuilt on existing site next to the first station that opened in 1867.

Barnet opened, costing £3.1 million and replacing the previous building built in 1903.

Leyton rebuilt on existing site and Lambeth river had new purpose built pontoon to replace older structure and now able to accommodate crews totally.

1992 Woodford rebuilt on existing site. Fulham fire station undergoing a £2 million refurbishment and building programme whilst keeping the Grade II listed building façade. A temporary building for one pump sited next door with the other pump located temporary at Chelsea fire station.

October Sanderstead FS closed.

1993. Islington rebuilt on existing site.

1994. Downham new appliance bay, watchroom etc, and offices built replacing old structure and adjoining the already replaced accommodation block previously old huts joined together.

Westminster under went a major refurbishment, the appliances being located at Lambeth FS during the work.

1995 July, Brigade changes the Command structure from five to three, Wembley Western, Stratford Eastern, Lewisham Southern, now including the introduction of Grouping of fire stations with Group Commanders.

1997. The Authority's Operations and Policy Resources Committee seek approval to lease part of a building at Heathrow Airport to house a pump ladder, previously a BAA fire station and then occupied by the LAS. This has come about because the central terminal area had been given an 'A' risk category in 1995 and it has been difficult for the brigade to meet the laid down attendance time.

1998. 20th March official opening of G56 Heathrow. 1st June, Barbican and Shooters Hill FS closed.

1999/2000. Authority Review of Fire Cover, report into fire cover in the Heathrow and Hayes area being drafted, with the proposal to introduce day manning at Purley fire station now abandoned and the possibility of a new fire station at Surrey Quays also abandoned. At the same meeting it was also decided to see if the private sector could help with providing property for stations prior to looking for sites for future new fire stations. Agreement was given to the start of projects to the refurbishment of Whitechapel fire station, the rebuilding of West Norwood fire station and the building of a new station to replace Hammersmith and one at The Isle of Dogs. It was also agreed to replace the present CMC building at present located at Lambeth HQ.

2000. New Authority for London. LFCDA goes and the LFEPA takes over. Following the Government decision to elect a Mayor for London, the people of London voted and elected Ken Livingstone to be the first Mayor elect for London.

During the time of the LFCDA, the brigade saw the change in management of the brigade fleet of appliances and the workshops and the issue of firekit to all firefighters. All these functions passed to private companies financed by the brigade under timed contracts. These companies would be responsible for the repair and collection of appliances and delivery of new appliances, whilst the company responsible for uniforms would supply repair or replace helmets, boots or tunics and leggings all of which meet today's high standards of safety and comfort for firefighters.

Ilford

AG collection
B1986
c1986
Station No. F42 North
East Area Command
1 – pump ladder
1 – pump
1 – Station Officer
1 – Sub Officer
1 – Leading Firefighter
10 – Firefighters

c2005
Station No. F42
Eastern Command
1 – pump ladder
1 – pump
1 – Station Officer
1 – Sub Officer
1 – Leading Firefighter
10 – Firefighters

Wimbledon

AG collection
B1988
c1988
Station No. H34 South
West Area Command
1 – pump ladder
1 – pump
1 – Station Officer
1 – Sub Officer
1 – Leading Firefighter
10 – Firefighters

c2005
Station No. E54
Southern Command
1 – pump ladder
1 –aerial ladder
platform
1 - IRU
1 – Station Officer
1 – Sub Officer
2 – Leading
Firefighters
12 – Firefighters

Peckham

B1991
c2005
Station No. E37 South
East Area Command

1 – pump ladder
1 – pump
1 – Station Officer
1 – Sub Officer
1 – Leading Firefighter
10 - Firefighters

Lambeth River pontoon

B1991
Lambeth river
c1985
part of South West
Area Command B22
Lambeth then became
E45 river using the
pontoon, and part of
Southern Command
and when fireboat
London Phoenix
replaced by Firedart
and Fireflash became
operational in Dec
1999 both rapid
response fireboats, one
with a dedicated crew
the other fireboat crew
from the pumps crew at
Lambeth, crews now
form part of the watch at
Lambeth station.

Barnet

B1991
C1991
Station No. A37 North
Area Command
1 – pump ladder
1 – pump
1 – Station Officer
1 – Sub Officer
1 – Leading Firefighter
10 – Firefighters

c2005
Station No. G54
Western Command
1 – pump ladder
1 – Sub Officer
1 – Leading Firefighter
5 – Firefighters

Leyton

B1991

c1991
Station No. F29
North East Area
Command
1 – pump ladder
1 – Sub Officer
1 – Leading Firefighter
5 - Firefighters

c2005
Station No. F29
Eastern Command
1 – pump ladder
1 – Sub Officer
1 – Leading Firefighter
5 – Firefighters

Woodford

B1992
c1992
Station No. J23 North
East Area Command
1 – pump ladder
1 – Sub Officer
1 – Leading Firefighter
5 – Firefighters

c2005
Station No. F35
Eastern Command
1 – pump ladder
1 - IRU
1 – Sub Officer
1 – Leading Firefighter
5 – Firefighters

Islington

Author's collection
B1993

c1993
Station No. A30
North Area Command
1 – pump ladder
1 – pump
1 – Station Officer
1 – Sub Officer
1 – Leading Firefighter
10 – Firefighters

c2005
Station No. F50
Eastern Command
1 – pump ladder
1 – pump
1 – Station Officer
1 – Sub Officer
1 – Leading Firefighter
10 – Firefighters

Downham

Author's collection
re-built appliance bay

c1993
South East Area
Command

c2005 part of Southern
Command station No.
E32

1 – pump ladder
1 – Sub Officer
1 – Leading Firefighter
5 – Firefighters

Heathrow

Author's collection
formerly Surrey FB &
BAA property.

C2005
Station No. G56
Western Command

1 – pump ladder
1 – Sub Officer
1 – Leading Firefighter
5 – Firefighter

Chapter 6

London Fire & Emergency Planning Authority (LFEPA) 2000-

2000, July new Authority commences with Ms Val Shawcross the first Chair to the new LFEPA.

December, at Authority meeting the go ahead given for plans to continue for the partnership with a private sector consortium to build a fire station on land at Byng Street Isle of Dogs, this will replace the existing Millwall FS. The station will have four appliance bays.

2001, The Authority has approved phase two of station improvements for 2001 / 2002 at a cost of £500, 000. Phase one which was carried out last year concentrated on improvements to stations where 30 fire women were posted, these station had no or poor separate facilities. This second phase that has already started will concentrate on 80 stations to improve toilets, showers wash areas and sleeping accommodation and changing facilities. Some stations will also have improved facilities for men.

2001 May, Authority now given their approval for the replacement of the Hammersmith FS with a new three - bay fire station to be built at 190 / 192 Shepherd's Bush Road. This new station will replace the old station at 244 Shepherd's bush Road, no longer suitable for today's modern fire brigade and will also accommodate in offices built above the station the Western Command Fire Safety staff, this will allow the Brigade to cease the lease on the building at present being used in Hounslow. The building will be carried out by Duffy Construction Ltd and will take approx 68 weeks to complete.

The Command structure ceased with the move of the ACO's back to HQ from their Commands.

Borough Stations which first began in 2000 as a pilot scheme will now become Brigade wide with Borough Commanders. The objective will be to work more closely with the Police, local Authorities and other agencies and for the public to have a local point of contact with the Brigade being able to call into a Borough station for advice and assistance.

2003. March Commissioner Brian Robinson retired from the Brigade and Deputy Commissioner Roy Bishop took temporary charge.

July, Chief Officer Ken Knight officially replaced Brian Robinson as the new Commissioner. Hammersmith moved to a new three bay Community fire Station in Shepherd's Bush Road. Bromley now has a fully operational community liaison office open to the public and outside agencies.

2004, Brigade control (CMC) moved to the new site at Docklands in May with the back-up at Stratford FS. With this move station numbers and appliance calls signs were re-organised as total Echo, Foxtrot and Golf eliminating those of Alpha and Hotel.

London is at the moment going through a change with an increase in appliance replacement including Fire Rescue Units to 10, and new additional appliances especially through the wake of terrorism and the possible threat to the London Capital. Incident response units 10 (IRU) and search and rescue units 2 (SRU) have now been placed on the run at selected stations a third will also be deployed, these are supplied by the Government. Some stations have manned up to crew them others are deployed with the PL using the station personnel to crew both. Also during 2004 the brigade fleet of aerial appliances also changed with the proposal of those at Chelsea, Dowgate, Islington, Leyton, Norbury and

Plaistow being removed with Dagenham due to receive an aerial appliance. Additional new aerials on Mercedes chassis are due, the fleet will be six Volvo and three Mercedes ALP's and two Dennis TL's with all HP's placed as reserve. The photos shown still show the establishment at current aerial stations.

2005 Manchester Square FS closed on 7th June, with station closures come job losses usually through natural wastage leaving because of sickness or retirement, but most firefighters are moved to other stations along with their appliances.

Millwall moved to their new station.

During the following months and into 2006 the brigade again will be making changes, for some time the brigade has proposed the changing of the existing staff offices, with the remaining functions being transferred to HQ, again this office may also move to Stratford FS, and more command units placed on the run at various stations, only time will tell if this comes about.

Fire stations will continue to be replaced when no longer able to fit in with today's modern requirements, these modern design stations offer better working, training and leisure facilities and others will be refurbished or facilities added as the community becomes more aware and involved with the Brigades role in fire safety in the community.

Several fire stations in London are located in areas where building land is very expensive and their sites are valuable such as Chelsea and Lambeth, both would probably be rebuilt with funding from private finance, Soho for example has been replaced using the original site and built as part of a commercial development. Other fire stations due for replacement could follow in the same way.

West Norwood will probably be rebuilt.

Although stations close they do not always disappear, dozens still exist under a different guise. Before any closing of stations it must be first confirmed that bordering stations that take over the fire ground, will be able to meet the Government's laid down attendance times to attend calls within the boundaries of the station closing, only then will a station close The London Fire Brigade is as always changing for the needs of the Brigade and the people of London.

LONDON FIRE BRIGADE BOUNDARY MAP

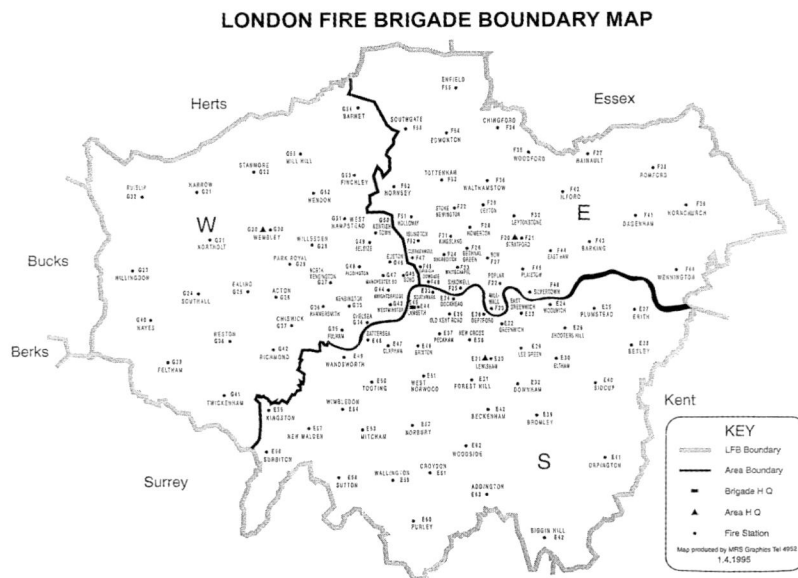

Hammersmith

Author's collection
B2003

c2005
Station No G36
Western Command
1 – pump ladder
1 – pump
1 – Station Officer
1 – Sub Officer
1 – Leading Firefighter
10 – Firefighters

Millwall

Author's collection

B2005 station No F23
Eastern Command

1 – pump ladder
1 – Sub Officer
1 – Leading Firefighter
5 - Firefighters

Appendix A

Listed Buildings of the London Fire Brigade as designated by English Heritage

1/.   Belsize Fire Station

2/.   Clerkenwell Fire Station

3/.   Euston Fire Station

4/.   Fulham Fire Station

5/.   Hammersmith Fire Station, now closed

6/.   Kensington Fire Station

7/.   Lee Green Fire Station

8/.   Manchester Square Fire Station now closed.

9/.   Millwall Fire Station, now closed and in new building.

10/.   Southwark Fire Station

11/.   Southwark Training Centre the Engine House Block

12/.   Southwark Training Centre, Winchester House

13/.   Tooting Fire Station

14/.   Wembley Fire Station

15/.   West Hampstead Fire Station

16/.   Shooters Hill Fire Station, now closed.

Appendix B

Stations refurbished or subject to major works (c2003)

1/. Full refurbishment.

Euston

Finchley

Fulham

Tooting

Twickenham

Westminster

Southwark Training Centre (excluding Fire station areas.)

2/. Partial refurbishment or extensions.

Downham

Eltham

Erith

Whitechapel

Acknowledgements

I would like to thank the following for their help with this book, it would not have been possible to obtain photos or information about the Brigade or even to edit or publish without them.

London Fire Brigade, The London Fire & Emergency Planning Authority.

Brian Robinson C.B.E. Q.F.S.M. Chief Officer of the London Fire Brigade 1991-2003

Gordon White Brigade Press Officer retired

Les Mardell Brigade HQ

Judy Seabourne Brigade Library retired

Graham De Core Brigade Library

Terry Jones Brigade Library
Photographic section RB

Pauline Drummond & Tanya Lloyd
Photographic section RB

Esther Mann Brigade Museum Southwark

Alan Gilfrin Stn O retired

Lambeth Borough Council Archives dept.

Captain B Mills

Eric Billingham Sub.O retired

Barbara my wife and Arran my son for all his help, especially the cover design.

About the Author

J.B. Nadal served with the London Salvage Corps from 1969–1974. He joined London Fire Brigade in 1974 and was posted to Lewisham Fire Station onto the blue watch, transferring in 1979 to the staff office at Lewisham HQ. Whilst there he redesigned the incident plan tally system, a system that was used on the control unit at Brigade HQ Lambeth. Following approval it was placed on all Brigade control units and was the back-up system when computers were first installed. Two other Brigades have used the system.

He transferred from Brigade HQ Lambeth to the COSG in 2000, and retired in December 2001.

This page: Lewisham GLC
Front Cover : Sydenham

www.jeremymillspublishing.co.uk

ISBN 0-9546484-7-1

9 780954 648473